blue
rider
press

THE *NEW* NEW RULES

THE *NEW* NEW RULES

A FUNNY LOOK AT

HOW EVERYBODY BUT **ME**

HAS THEIR HEAD UP THEIR ASS

BILL MAHER

BLUE RIDER PRESS

a member of Penguin Group (USA) Inc.   New York

blue
rider
press

Published by the Penguin Group
Penguin Group (USA) Inc., 375 Hudson Street, New York, New York 10014, USA •
Penguin Group (Canada), 90 Eglinton Avenue East, Suite 700, Toronto, Ontario M4P 2Y3, Canada
(a division of Pearson Penguin Canada Inc.) • Penguin Books Ltd, 80 Strand, London WC2R 0RL,
England • Penguin Ireland, 25 St Stephen's Green, Dublin 2, Ireland (a division of Penguin Books Ltd) •
Penguin Group (Australia), 250 Camberwell Road, Camberwell, Victoria 3124, Australia (a division of
Pearson Australia Group Pty Ltd) • Penguin Books India Pvt Ltd, 11 Community Centre, Panchsheel Park,
New Delhi–110 017, India • Penguin Group (NZ), 67 Apollo Drive, Rosedale, North Shore 0632,
New Zealand (a division of Pearson New Zealand Ltd) • Penguin Books (South Africa) (Pty) Ltd,
24 Sturdee Avenue, Rosebank, Johannesburg 2196, South Africa

Penguin Books Ltd, Registered Offices: 80 Strand, London WC2R 0RL, England

ISBN 978-1-61793-772-9

Printed in the United States of America

BOOK DESIGN BY MEIGHAN CAVANAUGH

Some portions of this material have appeared in slightly different form on HBO's *Real Time*,
in the *Los Angeles Times*, and on Salon.com and The Huffington Post.

While the author has made every effort to provide accurate telephone numbers and Internet addresses
at the time of publication, neither the publisher nor the author assumes any responsibility for errors,
or for changes that occur after publication. Further, the publisher does not have any control over
and does not assume any responsibility for author or third-party websites or their content.

To Jasmine

ACKNOWLEDGMENTS

Before we get to the fun stuff, I want to acknowledge and thank the people who make a project like this possible, fun, and painless.

David Rosenthal, the publisher of this tome. In 1993, I was on television for ten seconds when I asked this editor at Random House if that was credential enough to get my novel published. He saw a real book there, and I maintain to this day that *True Story* is a real book. I will forever be his fan for being my fan, and it's a pleasure to repay his faith all these years later with this cash cow.

Everyone at Penguin Books who has the savvy in actually assembling a book and marketing it, and, you know, grammar and stuff.

The *Real Time* writers who wrote so many of the jokes in this book: Chris Kelly, Brian Jacobsmeyer, Jay Jaroch, Matt Gunn, Adam Felber, and Danny Vermont. To do a once-a-week weekly wrap-up show like *Real Time* right, I need to come in to the office every day—though I wouldn't strictly need to have a writers' meeting every day. But why would I ever miss the most reliably fun and enlightening part of my day?

My invaluable team of producers, Sheila Griffiths, Scott Carter, and Dean Johnsen. Not only do they make the trains run on time, but they are such decent human beings it provides the essential counterbalance to the snarky host.

My script coordinator and keeper of records and dead bodies, Joaquin Torres, for the vital job of helping me to pull together, order, and edit the material for this book, all while somehow reading my handwriting. And sometimes my mind.

Real Time coproducer Matt Wood, for his outstanding work accessing, assembling, and sometimes creating the images for this book. My old job.

My longtime manager, Marc Gurvitz, and agent, Steve Lafferty, who had to do almost no work to sell this no-brainer of a cake project, but who have . . . oh, all right, at other times proven themselves useful.

My publicists, CeCe Yorke and Sarah Fuller, and everyone else at True Public Relations who does such a great job covering up all my scandals so as not to overshadow when I have something to sell.

From the executive suites of HBO, Nancy Geller—my Saint Peter, the rock upon which I built my church all those years ago (you know, metaphorically speaking)—and Richard Plepler and Mike Lombardo, who provide the real estate, and the nurturing of it, without which *New Rules* would just be a YouTube clip of a podcast of a tweet.

The fans! Duh . . . the people for whom I have such a special love because in a country that's gone as batshit crazy as this one, it is some comfort to know there are people who think in a similar fashion. By the way, anyone who comes up to me and says, "I watch you every night," you're not a real fan, because *I'm not on every night!*

And last but not least, Billy Martin is the *Real Time* head writer and the man who thought up the New Rules concept, and try as I might, I can't seem to cut him out of these books. Just as well, since he's the one who gits 'er done, with his usual creativity and ruthless efficiency.

THE *NEW* NEW RULES

FOREWORD

New Rule: People who read a book's foreword are anal. Especially this book's foreword. It's a joke book. What am I supposed to say? "Enjoy"? "Don't spill your Mr Pibb"? "Careful not to get a paper cut"? If you need a pep talk or some insight from me before diving in, maybe you're not ready for word books. Maybe you should stick to the kind of books that have pictures you can color.

Okay, I'm sorry. It's more than just a joke book, and I'm glad you took a moment to check in with me before proceeding. What you're holding is a collection of hundreds of my favorite New Rules and essays, some performed on the show and many others never before seen on TV—not because they suck, but for a variety of reasons, like: (a) it's a particularly filthy, dirty, potty-mouthed rule about fetish porn or edible panties or rhinoceros scrotums, and that week there was someone on our panel who would be appalled by it, like a congressman from a conservative district, or a clergyman. Or, you know, a woman.

Or (b) it might have been a terrific New Rule, but that week we had other good ones on the same subject. Although we have our share of viewers who are news junkies, I treat the show that we do live on Friday night as a catch-up show for those who might not have had the time during the week to see the news, because they work hard, have hobbies, or forgot to use birth control a couple of times in the '90s. So I try to cover as many of the important subjects as possible, either in the monologue, with the guests, or in the New Rules, and so it's survival of the fittest by topic.

Or (c) sometimes I read my writers' New Rules submissions completely baked and just picked the wrong ones.

As for the essays—or what we call our "editorial"—which are the much longer final New Rules that conclude the show: I can't lie, there are no new ones here; they were all done on the air. But, I must immodestly say, I think a lot of them bear repeating. They take three minutes to read on air, but I spend six or eight hours over the course of the week writing and editing them to get a show-ender that, I hope, both makes a unique point and does so in a funny way. It's the part of the show I'm most proud of and that I don't think you can see anywhere else on television. So please don't read this part of the book on the toilet or you'll break my heart.

And please know I'm not one of these celebrities who puts out a book every year or so to try and cash in on my fans' love and loyalty. That's what my line of meat marinades is for. And my Real Time, Real Smooth scented personal lubricant, now available at Walgreens.

I realize some celebrity books are like gnats or Anthony Weiner's penis, relentlessly coming at you and constantly in your face. My books are more like cicadas. They come out in longer intervals, Christians consider them a plague, and there's always at least one kid in the neighborhood who will eat one on a dare.

I try to make each book special. My last one was published in 2005, and the one before that in 2002. I think most men experience this: The older you get, the more time it takes you between releases.

So welcome to *The* New *New Rules: A Funny Look at How Everybody but Me Has Their Head Up Their Ass,* the second installment in my New Rules trilogy. I'm glad you picked it up, and I think you'll find it quite enlightening, especially chapter 7, where I describe in detail how Levi Johnston plied me with watermelon wine coolers and took my virginity in a tent. The sad part: Part of me still loves him.

Now, about the subtitle, *A Funny Look at How Everybody but Me Has Their Head Up Their Ass*. Truth is, I didn't even want to have a subtitle, but the publisher said these days in the book world it was de rigueur, like using a French phrase somewhere in the first ten pages to show you're a real "writer." The first *New Rules* book carried the subtitle *Polite Musings from a Timid Observer,* which cracked me up, but when promoting the book, I can count on my penis the number of times a morning deejay got the joke. You see, Fartface and Asshole Jack, I'm not *really* a timid observer, and my musings are known to be somewhat less than . . . oh, never mind.

So I took a more literal approach this time: "Everybody but me has their head up their ass"—I think we all feel that way sometimes! And that's why New Rules resonate with so many. They call out our fellow humans, providing that tug on the leash that urges them back to civil behavior. New Rules put a voice to life's gripes, everything from the petty annoyance of that little sticker on your supermarket plum to the brazen injustice of a Supreme Court that sides almost solely with corporations over individuals. Plus, it's the segment on my show when the panelists have to shut up and I get to talk.

As we approach the presidential election of 2012, it seems we need New Rules now more than ever. They're an attempt, albeit through humor, to bring at least some semblance of order to a world gone haywire. Do you realize we are currently overlooking the threat of climate change, which is more likely to be the end of us than anything else, while actively passing legislation to protect us from Sharia law? That's like ignoring the crackhead jimmying open your back door to confront the monster your toddler hears under her bed. Sure, you've assuaged a little girl's unfounded fear, but now you've got Tom Sizemore in your kitchen.

That's what this book is more than anything else: a pleasant, funny diversion, something to make you laugh while the earth slowly fries and suffocates in drought, wildfires, and eventual flooding that will engulf us all. I'm sorry, I meant it's fantastic beach reading and a terrific stocking stuffer.

While our politicians place personal power before patriotism, my New Rules are a call to consensus. They provide much-needed structure in an ever-changing world. And why not? We all live by rules, whether codified or implied. We adopt them through common sense (on the airplane, we'll exit row by row), common courtesy (at the gas station, we pull up to the far pump, so someone can pull in behind us), or experience (when sharing a cell, the bigger man gets his choice of bunks).

And then there are those rules we must simply learn for ourselves. For instance, when you're out shopping, you have to actually buy something. You can't just browse around endlessly, sniffing the merchandise and saying, "Mmm, I'm in heaven." Believe me, I've tried this, and eventually they ask you to leave the dispensary.

Finally, a word about time. I'm against it. Especially now that it seems to pass more quickly than ever. The world of 2005, when the first New Rules came out, seems as distant as Michele Bachmann's gaze when she talks about lightbulbs. We now have the iPad, Braille porn, cars that park themselves, and a new badass president who shoots pirates and terrorists in the face. Plus, the AMC network no longer shows just old movies. In paging through my previous New Rules book—and you really should pick it up; you wouldn't go see *Twilight: Eclipse* without having seen *Twilight: New Moon,* would you?—I couldn't help laughing at some of the new fads or conventions I poked fun at then, which are completely mainstream now. I railed on, for example, about the weirdos who walk around talking into those strange Bluetooth devices, and, of course, now Bluetooths come factory-installed on infants.

So enjoy these *New* New Rules now, while they're fresh. Because I find the world is changing much more quickly than I can bitch about it.

A

A CASE OF THE MUNDANES

New Rule: If you tweet neat stuff about your life for your friends to read more than ten times a day, I can tell you a neat fact about your friends: They hate you.

A FRIDGE TOO FAR

New Rule: The Internet doesn't have to be everywhere. Samsung has a new Internet-equipped refrigerator, just the thing for people tired of sending e-mail from their toaster. It's so convenient: Instead of writing an old-timey "analog" grocery list on paper, you simply command your iPod to talk to your refrigerator, which relays the request to your computer, and in six to ten working days a carton of milk will arrive from an Amazon .com warehouse facility in Nebraska, encased in six layers of Bubble Wrap. What could be easier?

AB FIVE FREDDY

New Rule: Stop posing with your shirt off on the cover of your hip-hop album. This look doesn't say gangsta. It says, "I'll suck your dick for some blow."

ACAPULCO SCOLD

New Rule: This one is for Mexican drug lords: If you don't knock off this violence right now, I'm going to stop smoking pot entirely. Just kidding. I'll get it from Thailand.

ACCOUNTS DECEIVABLE

New Rule: My bank must stop trying to sell me identity theft protection. You know why I expect you to protect my money? Because you're a *bank*. Besides, I've already taken the most important precaution to make sure nobody abuses my credit card: I'm single.

EVOLUTIONARY WAR

New Rule: You don't have to teach both sides of a debate if one side is a load of crap. President Bush recently suggested that public schools should teach "intelligent design" alongside the theory of evolution, because after all, evolution is "just a theory." Then the president renewed his vow to "drive the terrorists straight over the edge of the earth."

Here's what I don't get: President Bush is a brilliant scientist. He's the man who proved you could mix two parts booze with one part cocaine and still fly a jet fighter. And yet he just can't seem to accept that we descended from apes. It seems pathetic to be so insecure about your biological superiority to a group of feces-flinging, rouge-buttocked monkeys that you have to make up fairy tales like "We came from Adam and Eve," and then cover stories for Adam and Eve, *like intelligent design!* Yeah, leaving the earth in the hands of two naked teenagers, that's a real intelligent design.

I'm sorry, folks, but it may very well be that life is just a series of random events, and that there is no master plan—but enough about Iraq.

There aren't necessarily two sides to every issue. If there were, the Republicans would have an opposition party. And an opposition party would point out that even though there's a debate in schools and government about this, there is no debate among scientists. Evolution is supported by the entire scientific community. Intelligent design is supported by guys on line to see *The Dukes of Hazzard*.

And the reason there is no real debate is that intelligent design isn't real science. It's the equivalent of saying that the Thermos keeps hot things hot and cold things cold because it's a god. It's so willfully ignorant you might as well worship the U.S. mail. "It came again! Praise Jesus!"

Stupidity isn't a form of knowing things. Thunder is high-pressure air meeting low-pressure air—it's not God bowling. "Babies come from storks" is not a competing school of thought in medical school.

We shouldn't teach both. The media shouldn't equate both. If Thomas Jefferson knew we were blurring the line this much between Church and State, he would turn over in his slave.

As for me, I believe in evolution *and* intelligent design. I think God designed us in his image, but I also think God is a monkey.

—August 19, 2005

ACID REDUX

New Rule: Stop saying drug use makes people lazy. Jimi Hendrix did a lot of drugs, and even though he's been dead for forty years, he's *still* making new records. Suck on *that*, Partnership for a Drug-Free America! In fact, Jimi's new CD debuted at number four on the charts. Which tells me (a) his music is as relevant as ever . . . and (b) that baby boomers still haven't figured out how to steal music off the Internet.

ACID REFLUX

New Rule: Somebody who went to Woodstock has to admit that it sucked. Wow, you got to see Country Joe and the Fish, Sha Na Na, *and* Arlo Guthrie in one weekend? Plus you caught *E. coli* from having sex in the mud? I am soooo jealous! Let's look at the legacy of Woodstock. Tim Hardin? Heroin overdose. Janis Joplin? Heroin overdose. Jimi Hendrix? Choked on his own vomit. I can think of only one place I'd rather be, less than Woodstock: Woodstock '99.

ACTING BUG

New Rule: We don't need a Broadway musical about Spider-Man. He lives with his aunt, wears a body stocking, and leads a secret double life. He's gay enough already.

AFTER-DINNER HINT

New Rule: Waiters must stop saying, "Did you save room for dessert?" This is America. We don't save room for dessert, we make room for dessert. Dessert isn't a delightful way to cap off a meal, it's a challenge. In Russia they swim in subzero temperatures, in Spain they run with the bulls, and here we eat forty pounds of goo from a place called The Cheesecake Factory.

AIR BRAG

New Rule: If I can kick the back of the seat in front of me with my cock, I'm too close. Introducing the SkyRider, an airline seat that works like a saddle, so they can cram in more passengers. I don't mind shoving my bag under the seat, except when it contains my testicles.

AISLE BE BACK

New Rules: Don't grab a checkout-counter microphone, as someone recently did, and tell all the black people to get out of Whole Foods. One: It's racist. Two: It's not funny. Three: There are no black people in Whole Foods.

ALL SHALLOWS EVE

New Rule: Halloween must replace July Fourth as our National Holiday. Forget fireworks. Any day that combines spoiling children, corrosive food, and superstition says everything about this country anyone needs to know.

ALTITUDE ADJUSTMENT

New Rule: The kid behind me on the plane who's kicking my seat must put that energy to good use and beat the shit out of the kid in front of me on the plane who's playing peekaboo.

ANG LEE DIATRIBE

New Rule: Stop saying *Brokeback Mountain* lost Best Picture because of a homosexual backlash. The only homosexual backlash in Hollywood involves an actual homosexual literally hitting you on the back with a lash. Besides, if *Brokeback Mountain* taught us anything, it's that there's nothing wrong with coming in number two.

ANGEL DUST

New Rule: Your drug dealer and your priest should be two different dudes. An Illinois priest has been charged with operating a cocaine business out of his rectory. And you know how painful that can be. You think being *hit on* by your priest is unbearable, try having to talk to him for five hours because he can't get it up.

ANTI-HERO

New Rule: Now that Subway has passed McDonald's as the biggest franchise on earth, they need to change their name to something that doesn't make me think of a homeless guy pissing himself on the A train. Also, if you order your lunch by the foot, you should reexamine your relationship with food.

APP SMEAR

New Rule: Don't do that. Introducing Phone Fingers, a tiny rubber sheath that fits snugly over a finger—or, as they're called in Asia, condoms. Look, if either your phone or your finger has been somewhere so filthy you have to wear protection, nobody wants a call from you, anyway.

AQUA VULVA

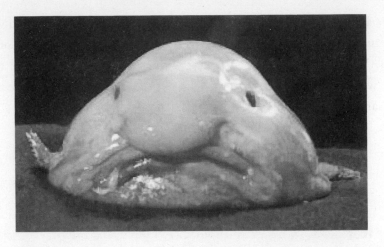

New Rule: This saltwater blobfish must be renamed the World's Saddest Vagina.

ARCH ENEMY

New Rule: You have to wear socks to the airport so the rest of us don't have to look at your stanky-ass feet in the security line. Seriously, between your stinky piggies and the obese lady in the stretch pants, how am I supposed to stay erect during my security pat-down?

ATTACK OF THE COLOGNES

New Rule: Old Spice will never be hip. Old Spice has introduced OS Signature for men. Yes, that same great scent from 1938 now in a spray bottle. Yeah, because that's what chicks dig—guys who smell like the uncle who molested them. "OS . . . like the men who wear it—a little too familiar."

AUTO NEUROTIC

New Rule: Valet parkers have to stop parking the swanky cars right in front of the restaurant while all the Toyotas and Fords get taken to a vacant lot six blocks away. We all know that America is a land of vast inequality; we don't need to be reminded of it by a Guatemalan immigrant in a red vest. Besides, the Maserati in front of the Olive Garden doesn't say, "This is a classy restaurant," it says, "Some coke dealer wants spaghetti."

AUTO NIX

New Rule: Since nobody reacts to car alarms anymore, stop putting alarms in cars. Face it. At this point, car alarms are like Glenn Beck: annoying, pointless, and everyone's finally learned to ignore them. When I hear one, my first thought is: "Please, God, I hope someone is stealing that car so they'll drive it away from my window."

SURREAL ESTATE

New Rule: Not to burst your bubble, but all bubbles burst.

I don't want to say real estate is overpriced these days, but I had a refrigerator delivered this morning and a homeless guy offered me three million for the box.

What's so distressing about this is that we just went through a bubble-bursting trauma with the dot-com crash, and here we are just five years later with real estate prices that could aptly be compared to Courtney Love: irrationally high and about to collapse.

Americans can no longer remember even recent history. Detroit has completely forgotten the lesson of the '70s, which was: When an oil crisis looms, stop making Godzillamobiles. In Iraq, George Bush totally forgot the lesson of Vietnam: Call Dad.

And yet, to be fair, it's not in the red states where this market insanity is most acute—it's among the supposedly savvy coastal elites, where buyers are dumping trillions into mortgages they can't afford, proving again just how much people will pay to *not* live in Kansas.

California is out of control: One property in San Diego sold five times in one day, with the price going up and up and up until it was just a picture of Donald Trump laughing.

But it won't be funny when the bubble bursts and people start going bankrupt, taking banks down with them, and then the markets and then the dollar, causing mass rebellion against the government—at which point the Republicans will run an election based on renaming Amtrak the Jesus Choo Choo—and win.

Because if there's one thing that Republicans schooled in the ways of Wall Street have taught us, it's this: Don't spend money you don't have.

Spend money *other* people don't have.

—August 26, 2005

B

BABY GAP SMEAR

New Rule: It's inhumane to put someone with special needs in front of a huge crowd. And it's also bad for the baby.

BABY POUTER

New Rule: The apparel industry must design some sort of "face bra" to lift and pull in John Boehner's lower lip.

BACHELOR PAD THAI

New Rule: Screenwriters have to think up a new cliché for single people other than the old carton of Chinese food in the refrigerator. According to every movie and TV show ever made, all single people have that one carton of Chinese food in their fridge, and then they smell it and recoil from the stench. And that's how we know they're single. How about this instead? Just show the character having sex. And that's how we know they're not married.

BAD FORM

New Rule: Online retailers must stop pestering me for "feedback." I'm a customer, not some chick you just boned. "How was it? Are you satisfied?" Shhh. Let's just lie here and not talk. Look, let me define our entire relationship: I type in my credit card number, you send me a big jug of Canadian Vicodin.

BAG MAN

New Rule: Science must get off its ass and invent a way for men to carry things without looking like morons. Why is it that I still have to choose between being the hippie with the backpack, the tool with the briefcase, or the doofus with the fanny pack? Besides, we already have a ridiculous-looking bag in which we carry our most prized possessions. It's called a scrotum.

BAIT EXPECTATIONS

New Rule: Getting up close and personal with sharks doesn't make you a wildlife enthusiast—it makes you dinner. An Austrian tourist wanted to get "face-to-face" with sharks, so he went diving in waters baited with bloody fish parts. And he got ate. A friend was asked to describe the man. He needed only two words: "Good chum."

BALLET FLOP

New Rule: Someone has to explain to me the difference between announcing the lineup for *Dancing with the Stars* and *Where Are They Now?* Just admit it, folks: You wanted to be relevant again, and it was between this and making a sex tape.

BARACK LIKE ME

New Rule: Stop saying Barack Obama isn't black enough. First you weren't sure America was ready for a black president. And now he's not black enough? "Hmm, I like his stand on the issues, but can he dunk?" Why are we even talking about him this way? Mitt Romney—

Now, *there's* someone who's not black enough to be president.

BAT OUT OF MATTEL

New Rule: The media must stop trying to excite me over Barbie's turning fifty. No offense to Cougar Barbie, but a disclaimer on the box says, "Ken comes separately."

BEARDED SHAM

New Rule: If you married a manic-depressive, three of your children died, and while you were president civil war broke out and someone shot you in the head, your coin really shouldn't say "In God We Trust."

TOWN HAUL

New Rule: Just because we have an obligation to rebuild New Orleans doesn't mean we have to put it back in the same place. Why don't we put it someplace where it can stay out of harm and do some good. After all, New Orleans is the Big Easy, and a lot of America is uptight. Which is why I say we put New Orleans in Kansas.

What do you say, Kansas—put down your hoes and come meet some. Welcome New Orleans to the land that fun forgot—an infusion of color and gayness in the dry Kansas plain. Why, it'll be as if they shot *The Wizard of Oz* on location.

You're gonna like it. New Orleans is one of the great towns. It's my kind of town—an outpost of free living and sophistication in a sea of . . . well, now, sea.

You can't tell me that the giant swath of Red America that Kansas sits in the middle of wouldn't benefit from thousands of insane Creoles who understand that hangovers happen only to people foolish enough to stop drinking. I read this week that the strippers have gone back to work in New Orleans. They don't even have clothes, and already they're taking them off. Kansas could use some of that spirit.

It could use some jazz, some blues . . . some blacks.

Don't think of it as a half-million black people moving in next door. Think of it as the *March of the Penguins*. Only, you know, with a half-million black people.

So what do you say, Kansas? They need a home. You need to get the stick out of your ass. It's a win-win. Come on, Kansas, show some curiosity. Show some compassion. But most of all, show us your tits!

—September 23, 2005

BED HEAD

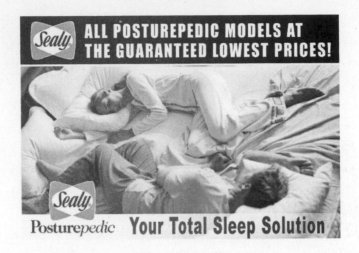

New Rule: Sealy Posturepedic must rewrite this ad to say what they really mean: "A mattress so comfortable, you'll doze off during 69."

BEDTIME FOR BRONZO

New Rule: If you're standing in front of a bronze statue, and you're bronzer, you're using too much bronzer.

BEER AS FOLK

New Rule: Next time, instead of taking a sip, chug. Chug the whole thing. You want to connect to white voters in middle America, Mr. President, knock that whole thing back, turn to that guy next to you, ask him what the fuck he's looking at, punch him in the face, call him a fag, then order a shot and do a karaoke version of "Don't Stop Believing" while riding the mechanical bull.

BET MEDDLER

New Rule: Just because you're the mayor and your team is in the World Series doesn't mean you have to make some horseshit bet with the other city's mayor, where you make him breakfast or eat a thousand chicken wings or let him watch your wife in the shower. You're the mayor. Not Mancow. And your team doesn't give a crap about Texas chili, or San Francisco crab cakes, or Cleveland steamers. Because they're all Dominican.

BETA BLOCKER

New Rule: Blockbuster can't announce it's closing 960 stores. Where will I go to rent a movie in 1988? And how do they still have 960 stores? Blockbuster, if you're still open next fall, you owe *me* a late fee.

BETTER FREIGHT THAN NEVER

New Rule: Airlines should just get it over with and start putting passengers in the cargo hold. Let's face it: You've already taken the legroom, the food, the pillows. The only thing left is to tag us, load us on that conveyor belt, and let us fight over who gets to sleep on the bag of mail.

BIEBER SHOT

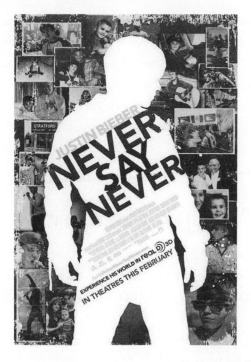

New Rule: If you're an adult and you go to the Justin Bieber movie by yourself and you're not a film critic, you have to register as a sex offender.

BINGE AND MERGE

New Rule: Halloween, Thanksgiving, and Christmas must be combined into one single super-holiday called Thanks-hallow-istmas. That way, you have to get together with your batshit family only once. In costume. For candy, presents, and a big turkey dinner. Then it's everybody into the den to watch football until your drunken uncle calls your cousin a whore.

THE BITCH SET ME UP

New Rule: Stop hitting on women at the dog park. Yes, we're talking to you, divorced guy with a ponytail. That better be a Milk-Bone in your pocket, because we're not glad to see you. Women come to the park to exercise their dogs, not to socialize with hounds. They wouldn't pick you up if they had a plastic bag on their hand. Although if you're determined to meet a woman at the dog park, here's a tip: Get a dog.

BITCHY & SCRATCHY

New Rule: Movie trailers have to stop indicating a comic reversal of fortune with the sound of a record scratch, because no one has scratched a record since 1985. For twenty-six years now, "vreeeeeeep" has been the sound of Owen Wilson losing his girlfriend, his job, and getting his dick caught in a car door. The record scratch is so obsolete, the thing that made it obsolete—the CD—is obsolete. But you can still keep using James Brown's "I Feel Good" for the part where Owen Wilson inherits a pet store and sings into a hairbrush. Because that never gets old.

BLOW 'N' TELL

New Rule: And this one is for the kids: Kids, if you're going to bring cocaine to class, make sure you bring enough for everyone. A second-grader in Philadelphia brought eighteen bags of cocaine to school and passed it around. Boy, there's a switch—going in the sandbox and getting crack in your sand. Then at recess one kid tried to fly a kite, but he'd done so much blow he couldn't get it up.

BODY SHOTS

New Rule: No more pictures of dead people in their coffins. It's a funeral, not a "Kodak moment." I don't want to remember Boris Yeltsin on his back, eyes closed and lifeless. I want to remember Boris Yeltsin how he lived: on his back, eyes closed and lifeless.

BONING IT IN

New Rule: There are double entendres, there are single entendres, and then there's Britney Spears's single "Hold It Against Me." What's her next song, "Put Your Penis in My Mouth"? She's a regular Cole Porter . . . and by that I mean, a long time ago, gay men liked her.

BOO, CAKEY

New Rule: Don't pretend Twinkies are healthy now, just because you can get the 100-calorie size. Here's the miracle: It's smaller. Here's how to make your own at home: Cut an old Twinkie in half. Here's how to make it healthy: Throw both halves in the toilet and eat a carrot.

BOWL MOVEMENT

New Rule: Froot Loops are not a health food. Some of the big food companies have started giving their products "Smart Choices" check marks so shoppers will know they're "healthful." You know, like a creep at the park will carry a puppy, so kids will know he's "friendly." Healthful? Froot Loops? When I saw this, *I* threw a tantrum in the cereal aisle.

BRAISEDHEART

New Rule: Just because the Scottish eat it, that doesn't make it food. The Obama administration has lifted the ban on imported haggis, a Scottish dish made from sheep's heart, liver, and lungs, and simmered in the sheep's stomach. Mmmm. But we already have that here. It's called a hot dog. Plus, their version looks disgusting, while ours is neatly pressed into the shape of a dog's hard-on. What I'm trying to say is: Buy American.

BREEDING RAINBOW

New Rule: Now that the army is letting in gays and lesbians, *Glee* has to add at least one character who's straight. Just for variety. My memories of high school are kind of fuzzy, but I'm pretty sure not every single human being in the building was gay. Television has an obligation to present America as it really is: ten percent gay. Ten percent real housewife. And seventy percent vampires.

BRISTOL-WHIPPED

New Rule: Bristol and Levi have to get back together. Come on, you two. You made the baby, fell out of love, and now it's act three of every horrible Katherine Heigl movie ever. It's the last scene, Bristol is plodding through one of her abstinence speeches. Suddenly Levi appears in the back of the room, and Bristol says, "Screw this! I love you, and I love sex!" They embrace, and the audience goes wild as they realize abstinence is just a big stupid joke in a world where you can wear a condom and fuck all you want. The end.

BUDDHA CON

New Rule: The fortunes in fortune cookies have to be fortunes. "You surround yourself with good friends" is not a prediction, it's a compliment. Quit kissing my ass, cookie. If I'm going to sit through a plate of MSG-laden twice-cooked kitty cat I want a real fortune, like "That meal you just ate is going to give you cancer."

THE BUG-EYE STATE

New Rule: Your sunglasses shouldn't be bigger than your head. When did looking fly mean looking like a fly? There's only one reason to wear sunglasses this big: cataract surgery. You don't look sexy, you look like a transvestite Larry King.

BUMBLE PIE

New Rule: Since we're running out of bees and being overrun with bedbugs, scientists must breed a bedbug that shits honey. It can't be worse than Splenda. Oh, right, like that's so much grosser than where we get silk and eggs. Ask for it by name: Bedbug Ass Honey: For When You're Itching for Something Sweet™.

BUZZ ALTERIN'

New Rule: The women's vibrator industry has to get back to basics. What is this thing? Does it make you have an orgasm or water your plants? Do I use it to play Xbox? Do I speak into it? And why is everything named after rabbits? Jack Rabbit, Power Rabbit, Rabbit Ears, Wascally Rabbit, Bunny Love, Water Bunny, Bunny Honey. I'd buy you one, but I'm worried you'll get rabies.

SENIOR, BITE US

New Rule: When a woman over sixty has a baby, it's not a miracle from God. It's a miracle from genetic engineers, fertility experts, and the good people at Merck. Here in California, a sixty-two-year-old woman, with eleven children, twenty grandchildren, and three great-grandchildren, gave birth. Again. To a forty-year-old man who walked out. At an age when most women are content to putter around the garden or perform the opening number at the Grammys, Janice Wulf, age sixty-two, told the press at a news conference, "Age is a number. Every time you revolutionize something, there's going to be naysayers." To which the reporters replied, "We're over here."

And lady, you're not a revolutionary. You're a vagina with no off switch. Twelve kids? Lemme guess: You're either a Catholic or a hamster.

Look, I don't want to be the one to say that this lady is too old and she's already had enough children, but this lady is too old and she's already had enough children! Hey, when you're sixty-two and you want children, you have two choices: (a) in vitro fertilization, or (b) luring them into a house made out of candy.

I wouldn't make such a big thing out of it, but it turns out Mrs. Wulf is not the first over-sixty-year-old to have a baby in the last decade—there is a virtual epidemic of granny sluts who insist on squeezing out children who, when they get a little older, will face many uncomfortable moments, like when it's parents' day at school and the kid shows up with an urn.

Why is creating life, under any conditions whatsoever, so applauded when there are already millions of unwanted kids around the world? And Angelina Jolie can't save them all. In fact, someone's gotta tell Angie that sometimes when you go to a foreign country—it's okay just to bring home a T-shirt.

—February 24, 2006

C

CALL GRRR

New Rule: If I called you, and our call gets dropped, *I call you back!* See, because if you're re-calling me while I'm trying to re-call you, we both go to voicemail. Which—to be honest—I was hoping to get in the first place.

CALLING PAN

New Rule: It's okay for AT&T and T-Mobile to merge, just so long as they retain the individual qualities of each company: frequently dropped calls *and* phantom charges on my bill. Also, they must develop an app that tells the chick texting in the car in front of me that *the light has turned green.*

CANNED HAM

New Rule: On the next season of *The Apprentice,* Donald Trump has to fire himself. His casinos are bankrupt. The only industry in the world where people give you money in exchange for nothing, and he blew it. Seriously, Choctaw Indians can make this work.

CANNED JOB

New Rule: Instead of killing 99.9 percent of germs, Lysol has to just go ahead and kill them all. Why spare the remaining 0.1 percent? So they can return to their villages and tell the other germs, "Dude, do not mess with Lysol"?

CAR BERATER

New Rule: Hey, car, you know that light you keep on for a few minutes after I park? You can go ahead and shut that off when I close the door. Why keep it on? Denial? Because you miss having me inside you? I'm gone. Why does everything have to be a process? I'm getting out of my car, not pulling out of Iraq.

CARDINAL SIN

New Rule: Birdwatchers have to wear uniforms so I don't mistake them for perverts trying to peep in my windows. Look, I'm sorry I chased you down the street naked and screaming—I thought you were TMZ. Can't we let bygones be bygones and agree to drop the charges? Look on the bright side: For a bunch of octogenarians, you ladies sure can run.

CARGO KIDDER

New Rule: Spirit Airlines, the airline that wants to charge for carry-on baggage, must merge with . . .

. . . Ryanair, the airline that wants to charge for using the washroom, and form a new carrier:

CELL MATE

New Rule: If this device tracks my every move, down to the second, but it still won't let me talk, it's not a phone, it's a woman.

HYPE-OCHONDRIA

New Rule: Drug companies have to stop making up diseases. I don't know what the terrorists are planning next for America, but if I had every problem they talk about in medicine commercials—breathing, lifting, walking, sitting, sleeping, crapping, not crapping, getting a boner, and male pattern menopause—I'd welcome death. Bring it on. Deadly nerve gas? Please, I've got seasonal allergies!

It seems like every time I turn on the TV these days I see some ad for some drug I never heard of to treat some disease I never heard of. That's not a stomachache you have from eating the chili-cheese fries at Johnny Rockets, it's irritable bowel syndrome, or IBS. Or, as I call it, BS. Which would also apply to the dreaded social anxiety disorder, or, as we used to call it, shyness—and we treated it with an old home remedy: scotch and water.

Your wife doesn't get turned on? It couldn't be because you're a snowman-shaped sausage casing so full of beer you sweat hops. It's because she has female sexual dysfunction. And before they came up with restless leg syndrome, did it even exist? Did you ever hear someone say, "Sorry I couldn't make the party, Bill, the old restless leg was acting up"?

I'm waiting for the ad that tells me my morning hard-on is actually superfluous rigidity syndrome, or SRS, and has a cartoon bunny who says, "Are you bothered by morning stiffness? Try Flaccidix. Flaccidix is specially formulated to make your penis shiny and more manageable. Side effects? You bleed from your pores, then explode and die. And/or dry mouth."

—April 28, 2006

CHAI NOON

New Rule: Gun-control people have to stop pressuring Starbucks to ban guns. I want my gun nuts overcaffeinated, twitchy, and accident-prone. That way, the problem will take care of itself. Plus, if just one gun nut kills just one pseudo-intellectual writing a screenplay-slash-graphic-novel on his iPad, natural selection is doing its job.

CHAIN OF FOOLS

New Rule: The next clever thing you invent that conveniently fits on my keychain must be a device that helps me *lift my keychain.* Thanks to the dongle that unlocks my car, the gadget that stores my computer files, and the dingus that gives me my supermarket discounts, I'm now the dorkus who can barely get my keys into my pocket. And no, geeks, that bulge in your pants doesn't make you look cool. It makes you look like you have a Swiss Army penis.

CHICK CORNEA

New Rule: Don't keep the Super Glue next to your eye drops. An elderly woman in Phoenix was reaching for her cataract medicine and—yes, she Super Glued her eyes shut. And after seeing what happened, her husband of many years took the Super Glue and moved it next to the toothpaste.

CHIME AND PUNISHMENT

New Rule: Churches have to stop ringing the damn bells. It was a good idea in the Middle Ages, but people have clocks now. It's not like you're doing us all a favor by keeping the hunchbacks off the street. Make up your mind, are you a house of worship or an ice cream truck?

CHINA FILL-UPS

New Rule: You can mess with your friends when they pass out, but not in the ass. When a Chinese man passed out drunk, his friends thought it'd be funny if they placed a live eel in his rectum. And then it gnawed through his guts and he died. The worst part of this story? That's how they make moo goo gai pan.

CHOP STICKLERS

New Rule: Waiters in Asian restaurants have to stop giving me attitude when I ask for a fork. It's not a hate crime, you know. Now, if you'd please, I'd like to get that food you just put in front of me into my stomach before it dawns on me what the fuck it is.

CHROME LIMBS

New Rule: Stop with Michelle Obama's arms. Women were clamoring for the issue of *Women's Health* magazine in which Michelle's trainer tells how you can get her guns in just nine minutes a day. But I don't buy that, because First Lady Laura Bush's arms never got that cut, and she spent eight years holding on to a dumbbell.

CHUBBY CHECKER

New Rule: Before telling me all about your Let's Move healthy-schools program, you have to explain why the kid in your poster has an erection.

CLAMBER ALERT

New Rule: The shirtless douche bag who climbs up on a light post at every spontaneous street celebration must be Tasered immediately. No one is thinking, "Hey, look at that guy high above the rest of us—he's our leader." We're all thinking, "Why'd he wear shorts? I can see his nuts."

CLASP WARFARE

New Rule: When the news story about record home foreclosures is followed immediately by the story about Victoria's Secret's new $2 million jewel-encrusted bra, maybe it *is* time to redistribute the wealth. The bra contains 1,542 carats of white diamonds, blue sapphires, and blue topaz set in 18-carat white gold. And yet it's *still* an annoying eyesore when you leave it hanging over the shower rod.

CLASS ACTION

New Rule: Scientists must tell us what's in Tampa's drinking water that makes teachers want to fuck their students. Remember Debra Lafave of Tampa? Well, three more Tampa schoolmarms have been arrested for having sex with kids in their class. Authorities are warning parents to look for telltale signs of an affair, like a sudden change in your child's behavior or a note on his report card that says, "Tommy is a pleasure to have in my vagina."

CLAYDAR

New Rule: You can't call it coming out of the closet when the door was wide open, the closet was made of glass, and everyone could see you in there having gay sex. Clay Aiken says he came out because he didn't want to lie to his infant son. Dude, even the baby knew you were gay. I can't wait to see next week's issue of *People*.

CLERK BAR

New Rule: The lady at the drugstore doesn't have to wear a lab coat. You're not Madame Curie, and I'm not shopping for radium. With all due respect, professor, I just want some beer and some Slim Jims, and everywhere else was closed.

CLOTHES CALL

New Rule: Ed Hardy fashions need more shit going on. When I run into someone in an Ed Hardy getup, I don't know whether to compliment his style or start looking for Waldo.

CLUB FOR GROWTH

New Rule: California, the state with the most debt and the most marijuana dispensaries, must be allowed to avoid bankruptcy by selling weed to neighboring states. That's how we'll get out of this budget crisis—by holding a "baked sale." It's the perfect solution. We need the cash . . . and Arizona needs to chill the fuck out.

CLUELESS

New Rule: The person who sat in my seat on the flight before me and could not finish the *People* magazine crossword puzzle has to be ashamed of themselves. I don't know who you are, but "Desperate _____wives"? Nothing? A three-letter word for "Writing utensil, you're holding it in your hand." Here's one more for you: Four letters, begins with a *v*, something you shouldn't be allowed to do this November.

COIF DROP

New Rule: If you see me every day and then I get a haircut, you don't have to ask me, "Hey, did you get a haircut?" No. No. I'm the one person on the planet whose hair grows in reverse. And in a completely neat and uniform way. Isn't that weird? I'm like the Benjamin Button of hair. I've been to the Mayo Clinic, Mass General, Johns Hopkins—no one can figure it out. And now they want to call the condition Maherism. But who wants to be remembered that way? As a man whose hair grew back into his head every six weeks or so? Whose hair will one day grow all the way into my brain and then come out my eyeballs. Oh, the shame of it! Please, oh, vengeful God, take me now! . . . Yes, I got a haircut.

COLLECTILE DYSFUNCTION

New Rule: Scientists must explain why we will stop and watch a movie on cable even though we own that exact same movie on DVD and could watch it anytime we want. I call it *Shawshank* syndrome, and I've realized DVDs are a lot like marriage. When it's there every single night just sitting right in front of you . . . for some reason, you don't feel like putting it in.

COLOR COMMENTARY

New Rule: It's okay for a black man to be the dumb guy in a commercial. It seems like in every commercial on television it's always the black guy who knows the fastest wireless network, knows the best car-rental company, knows the best place to buy music. Black people aren't always smarter than white people. It just sometimes seems that way by comparison.

COME ON, STYRENE

New Rule: Stacking cups is not a sport. ESPN has been airing the World Sport Stacking Championships, where kids stack and unstack pyramids of plastic cups at lightning speed. It's all the pageantry of Little League combined with all the suspense of watching someone unload a dishwasher. Here's how you know a skill isn't really a sport: when "turning pro" means you're a barback.

COMPUTER CRASH

New Rule: Instead of getting me the new steering-wheel desk for my birthday, save the $19.99 and just write "I hope you die" on a card.

CONDOMNATION

New Rule: Condoms are not sex toys. Trojan has released a new line of condoms that vibrate and heat up. Look, condoms keep people from getting AIDS and the clap. Haven't they done enough? You want to improve condoms? Invent a wrapper guys can open before they lose their hard-on.

CORDON BLEW

New Rule: Celebrity chefs have to get over themselves. At Mario Batali's new $12 million New York City eatery, he's serving a pasta dish with black truffles, cockscombs, and duck testicles. Okay, I'm trying to eat dinner, not pledge a fraternity. Though I must admit: The spit-roasted Latvian mongoose wrapped in the saffron-encrusted gingerweed served in a fifteenth-century Aztec war mask was *to die for.*

CORK BLOCKER

New Rule: Don't bring wine to my dinner party. Because then if you drink it, it's not really a gift, is it? But if I choose a different wine, you're thinking, "What the hell's wrong with the bottle I brought?" And when you bring wine and then say, "I don't drink," what kind of condescending crap is *that*? Your cute little gift is such a minefield of potential awkwardness; thank God I'm already high.

CORN ON MACABRE

New Rule: Don't try and make the boring parts of a horror movie scary by having someone—who's not the killer—jump out and scare someone "just for fun." It's like making a porn movie where a hot-looking maid enters the scene and you think she's going to blow you, but it turns out she's just there to dust.

COURSE LOAD

New Rule: College students are allowed to masturbate. Towson University forced the editor of the student paper to resign after he ran a column about masturbation. I don't know what's sadder: that colleges can still be this squeamish or that college kids need to be taught how to rub one out. Besides, when it comes to jerk-off columnists, you just can't beat George Will.

COUTURE CLASH

New Rule: You can't wear a Che Guevara T-shirt with your designer jeans, unless you're trying to be ironic. One is a symbol for impoverished workers, the other was sewn by them. You want to support the poor people in Latin America? Buy more coke.

PRIDE OF THE YANKEES

New Rule: America must stop bragging it's the greatest country on earth, and start acting like it. I know this is uncomfortable for the "faith over facts" crowd, but the greatness of a country can, to a large degree, be measured. Here are some numbers. Infant mortality rate: America ranks forty-eighth in the world. Overall health: seventy-second. Freedom of the press: forty-fourth. Literacy: fifty-fifth. Do you realize there are twelve-year-old kids in this country who can't spell the name of the teacher they're having sex with?

America has done many great things. Making the New World democratic. The Marshall Plan. Curing polio. Beating Hitler. The deep-fried Twinkie. But what have we done for us lately? We're not the freest country. That would be Holland, where you can smoke hash in church and Janet Jackson's nipple is on their flag.

And sadly, we're no longer a country that can get things done. Not big things. Like building a tunnel under Boston, or running a war with competence. We had six years to fix the voting machines; couldn't get that done. The FBI is just now getting e-mail.

Prop 87 out here in California is about lessening our dependence on oil by using alternative fuels, and Bill Clinton comes on at the end of the ad and says, "If Brazil can do it, America can, too!" Since when did America have to buck itself up by saying we could catch up to Brazil? We invented the airplane and the lightbulb, they invented the bikini wax, and now they're ahead?

In most of the industrialized world, nearly everyone has health care and hardly anyone doubts evolution—and yes, having to live amid so many superstitious dimwits is also something that affects quality of life. It's why America isn't gonna be the country that gets the inevitable patents in stem cell cures, because Jesus thinks it's too close to cloning.

Oh, and did I mention we owe China a trillion dollars? We owe everybody money. America is a debtor nation to Mexico. We're not on a bridge to the twenty-first century, we're on a bus to Atlantic City with a roll of quarters. And this is why it bugs me that so many people talk like it's 1955 and we're still number one in everything.

We're not, and I take no glee in saying that, because I love my country, and I wish we were, but when you're number fifty-five in this category, and ninety-two in that one, you look a little silly waving the big foam "number one" finger. As long as we believe being "the greatest country in the world" is a birthright, we'll keep coasting on the achievements of earlier generations, and we'll keep losing the moral high ground.

Because we may not be the biggest, or the healthiest, or the best educated, but we always did have one thing no other place did: We knew soccer was bullshit. And also we had the Bill of Rights. A great nation doesn't torture people or make them disappear without a trial. Bush keeps saying the terrorists "hate us for our freedom," and he's working damn hard to see that pretty soon that won't be a problem.

—*October 27, 2006*

CRACKER SHOT

New Rule: Hillbillies can't have computers. In Florida, a man named Joseph Langenderfer was so annoyed at his son for spending all his time playing computer games that he fired a gun at the computer. And if that's not stupid enough, he *missed*. And you call yourself a Langenderfer? Come on, Joe, even Dick Cheney could hit a Dell Dimension from a distance of zero feet. When your patron saint Elvis shot at Robert Goulet on the TV, he *hit* Robert Goulet, he didn't miss and wing a velvet painting. There's nothing I hate more than a redneck that won't make the effort to be the best redneck he can be.

CRASS REGISTER

New Rule: No more gift registries. It used to be just for weddings. Now it's for babies and new homes and graduations from rehab. Picking out the stuff you want and having other people buy it for you isn't gift giving. It's the white-people version of looting.

CREDIT CANARD

New Rule: Stop saying "we" got Osama. "We" didn't do anything. "We" were watching *The Celebrity Apprentice* and eating Funyuns in our sweatpants. SEAL Team 6 did the killing, with money we borrowed from Beijing, which our grandchildren will have to pay back. So it was a joint Navy SEALs/People's Bank of China/grandchildren operation.

CROCKTAIL

New Rule: An appletini is not a martini. A martini is gin, vermouth, and an olive. An appletini is just something a sex predator invented to hide the taste of the roofie.

CRULLER INTENTIONS

New Rule: I don't know how to fix the "donut hole" in Medicare, but the first step to better health might be: Stop seeing everything as a donut.

CUERVO GOLD

New Rule: You can't get mad about Applebee's serving a toddler a margarita unless you've ever tried to eat at Applebee's sober. That's right, some kid was served what can only be called a "Very Happy Meal," and nobody noticed until he started yelling, "Wait, hold up, this is my jam!" Here's how you can tell you're in a bad restaurant: When you call an ambulance and ask it to pick you up around the corner, at Chili's.

D

DAFFY FUCK

New Rule: Guys have to stop saying that crazy women are the best in bed. I'm sorry, but half an hour of great sex does not make up for twenty-three and a half hours of weeping, setting the pillows on fire, and coming at you with a butcher knife. And conversely, women have to stop saying the best sex is with "bad boys." If that's true, then why aren't you fantasizing about Goldman Sachs CEO Lloyd Blankfein?

DAIRY ERR

New Rule: Americans have to come up with a better cheese to represent the nation than American cheese. I'm not even sure American cheese is cheese. I think it's aged Jell-O. And it doesn't need to be individually wrapped in plastic, either. You're thinking of condoms.

DAS BOOTY

New Rule: She gained weight; she lost weight. She's playing an illiterate with an accent in a Holocaust movie. She's taking her clothes off in harsh light, crying, wearing old-lady makeup. For the love of God, can we give Kate Winslet her Oscar so we can all get on with our lives?

New Rule: If you dragged your man to *Eat, Pray, Love* this summer, he gets to take you to a movie called *Football, Jerk Off, Nap.*

DEAR ABBY

New Rule: You can't publish a book if the only people interested in reading it don't know how to read. *Jersey Shore*'s Mike "The Situation" Sorrentino has a new book out, which raises the question, can you get herpes from a book?

THE DEAR HUNTER

New Rule: If you give a nine-year-old a hunting rifle, expect to have a hole in your head next to the one you already have. That's right, fathers are signing up their kids to win free hunting trips. Great time to find out she's pissed about not getting that doll. I'm sorry, but the first time your daughter should see a shotgun is at her wedding when she's fourteen.

DEATH TO POOCHY

New Rule: Don't feel bad that the Taco Bell Chihuahua died. Yes, the Taco Bell Chihuahua has gone to his great reward in the ground. Oddly enough, the cause of death? Taco Bell. But don't worry, fans. If you would like to visit the dog's remains, just order a Burrito Grande.

DELAY OF GAME

New Rule: No offense, honey, but just shut up and open the case. Look, you're eye candy with an opposable thumb. So drop the dramatic pause and the chitchat. If I wanted to be frustrated by a half-dressed chick while a fortune slips away, I'd go to the Spearmint Rhino.

ORWELL THAT ENDS WELL

New Rule: Liberals must stop saying President Bush hasn't asked Americans to sacrifice for the war on terror. On the contrary, he's asked us to sacrifice something enormous: our civil rights. When I heard George Bush was reading my e-mails, I probably had the same reaction you did: "George Bush can read?" Yes, he can, and this administration has read your phone records, credit-card statements, mail, Internet logs—I can't tell if they're fighting a war on terror or producing the next season of *Cheaters*. I mail myself a copy of the Constitution every morning just on the hope they'll open it and see what it says.

So when it comes to sacrifice, don't kid yourself: You *have* given up a lot. You've given up faith in your government's honesty, the goodwill of people overseas, and six-tenths of the Bill of Rights. Here's what you've sacrificed: search and seizure, warrants, self-incrimination, trial by jury, cruel and unusual punishment; here's what you have left: handguns, religion, and they can't make you quarter a British soldier. If Prince Harry invades the Inland Empire, he has to bring a tent.

In previous wars, Americans on the home front made a very different kind of sacrifice. During World War II, we endured rationing, paid higher taxes, bought war bonds. In the interest of national unity, people even pretended Bob Hope was funny. Women donated their silk undergarments so they could be sewn into parachutes—can you imagine nowadays a Britney Spears or a Lindsay Lohan going without underwear? Okay, bad example.

George Bush has never been too bright about furreners, but he does know Americans. He asked this generation to sacrifice the things he knew we wouldn't miss: our privacy and our morality. He let us keep the money. But he made a cynical bet that we wouldn't much care if we became a "big brother" country that has now tortured a lot of random people. And yet no one asks the tough questions, like: "Is torture necessary?" "Who will watch the watchers?" and "When does Jack Bauer go to the bathroom?" It's been five years; is he wearing one of those astronaut diapers?

After 9/11, President Bush told us Osama bin Laden could run but he couldn't hide. But then he ran, and hid, so Bush went to plan B: pissing on the Constitution.

Conservatives always say the great thing Reagan did was make us feel good about America again. Do you feel good about America now? I'll give you my answer, and to get it out of me, you don't even have to hold my head under water and have a snarling guard dog rip my nuts off. No, I don't feel very good about that. They say that evil happens when good men do nothing. And the Democrats prove it also happens when mediocre people do nothing.

—March 16, 2007

DELLBERT

New Rule: You're never going to pick up women at a coffee shop pretending to be working on your laptop. You don't look like you're sensitive; you look like you're homeless. The last guy to pick up a chick with an Apple was Adam. And when you sit across from another dateless loser with a laptop, it still doesn't look like you're working—it looks like you're playing Battleship.

DESPICABLE HE

DICK MORRIS
"CATASTROPHE" AUTHOR
Hannity

New Rule: After Sean Hannity brings on Dick Morris, he has to give us time to go wash. It's like someone took everything that's wrong with politics, partisanship, cable news, personal hygiene, masculinity, humanity, and reality, and squeezed it into one man. I know he once kept a paid mistress so he could suck on her toes, but trust me, that's the least scummy thing this guy has ever done. Dick is the type of guy who's somehow always in the bathroom when the check arrives. But not just because he's a cheap liar. It's also because there's free gum in the urinals.

DESSERT CARP

New Rule: If I can't suck your milkshake through a straw, it's not a milkshake—it's a glass of ice cream. Now blend it again, Welcome-to-Baskin-Robbins-My-Name-Is-Kevin. And this time, give it a minute. You're in a pink-and-brown smock—it's not like you have a date later.

DIAL TOME

New Rule: Stop bringing me the phone book. The last time anyone even needed a phone book was 1988. And that was a cop using it to beat a suspect.

DICK CAVEAT

New Rule: If somebody asks if you tweeted your penis and your answer is anything other than "No," you tweeted your penis. Congressman Weiner, you're one of the only Democrats in Congress with balls. We knew that. You didn't have to e-mail proof.

DINGO STAR

New Rule: For at least the next generation, the Crocodile Hunter clan has to leave nature alone. This week, the late Steve Irwin's youngest son was bitten by a boa constrictor. Authorities don't know exactly what went wrong, but they think the accident might have happened when a bunch of idiots let a four-year-old fuck around with a giant snake. This isn't zoology, it's a family feud with fauna. I'm not saying Britney Spears was Mother of the Year—but she never let anyone get bitten by a snake, and she used to wear one around her neck.

DIXIE CHIC

New Rule: This year, the South gets to have all the one hundred fiftieth anniversary of the Civil War celebrations they want, but after that they have to let it go. The rest of us have moved on. Ken Burns has moved on. I know your great-grandpappy fought in the War of Northern Aggression and it had absolutely nothing to do with slavery, but (a) you're wrong, and (b) I didn't come to this bathhouse for conversation.

DL, HUGELY

New Rule: Never let your children take an overnight trip with a holy man who wears more than two pieces of jewelry. Atlanta's Bishop Eddie Long has been accused of buying cars for teenage boys, then inviting them to New Zealand and molesting them, in what authorities are calling "the worst Oprah surprise of all time." Which leads me to: New Rule: If your minister says being gay is bad, or a sin, or an evil temptation, or has any opinion on it stronger than "Who gives a shit?" then your minister is gay.

DOC JOHNSON

New Rule: If your doctor pulls on rubber gloves and then a condom, there's something wrong. An Oregon woman is suing her doctor, claiming he had intercourse with her as "treatment" for her lower-back pain. Call me a traditionalist, but I prefer when doctors screw their patients the old-fashioned way—by giving them the bill.

DOGGIE STYLE

New Rule: If your dog has to dress up like a human on Halloween, then you have to sleep on the floor naked and drink out of the toilet. Or, as Andy Dick calls it, "Saturday."

DOGS PLAYING POKE 'ER

New Rule: Tiger Woods, Jesse James, and Charlie Sheen must have a whore-off. It's like Hungry Hungry Hippos—you know, if eating all those marbles gave the hippos hepatitis C. Winner gets $100,000, a Cadillac Escalade, and a new beautiful, trusting bride, who is convinced you've changed, you're finally ready to settle down, and dammit, you mean it this time! . . . Even though you just won *the whore-off*.

D'OHPEC

New Rule: America has every right to bitch about gas prices suddenly shooting up. How could we have known? Oh, wait, there was that teensy, tiny thing about being warned constantly over the last forty years but still creating more urban sprawl, failing to build public transport, buying gas-guzzlers, and voting for oil company shills. So, New Rule: Shut the fuck up about gas prices.

DON'T TREAD ON WEE-MAN

New Rule: Anyone who whines about America losing its freedoms must watch any *Jackass* movie. This is a country where you can still Super Glue a midget to a fat guy and set off fireworks inside your ass. If that's cramping your style, Tea Baggers, then move to Holland.

DOS ICKIES

New Rule: Stop calling bagpipes a musical instrument. They're actually a Scottish Breathalyzer test. You blow into one end, and if the sound that comes out the other end doesn't make you want to kill yourself—you're not drunk enough.

DOUBLE DRIVEL

New Rule: Now that it's been declared unconstitutional, we must change the name of the National Day of Prayer to the National When You Wish upon a Star Day. Seriously, what's the difference? You know, other than that stars are real.

DREAMS FROM MY FODDER

Act goes awry, human cannonball dies

April 25, 2011 | By Tom Watkins, CNN

Share Mixx Twitter Email

Recommend 1,996 people recommend this.

A man who was taking part in a human cannonball show in Detling, England, was fatally injured Monday when the event failed to go off as planned, Kent police said.

The incident occurred in the afternoon during Scott May's Daredevil Stunt Show at the Kent County Showground, southeast of London, police said.

The British Press Association, citing police, said a safety net failed to engage.

A Kent Police spokesman declined to identify the man beyond saying he was in his 20s. Relatives of the man had been informed of the mishap, but his body had not been formally identified, a police spokesman said.

New Rule: When a human cannonball dies, it's not a tragedy. It's a finale.

DRILL, MAYBE, DRILL

New Rule: Stop calling Sarah Palin a "babe." Megan Fox is a babe. Sarah Palin is a pleasant-looking forty-six-year-old woman in mom jeans. Is this really all it takes to give America a hard-on? This . . .

. . . is the first lady of France. I repeat, this is the first lady of France. And we're excited about some Pentecostal nitwit in an L.L.Bean parka?

DUDE AWAKENING

New Rule: Stop putting "Bro" in front of everything. Bromance, bro-down, brodak moment. Way to make shoe shopping with my friend Steve sound gay. Oh, and one way to tell your "bromance" has grown into a full-on gay relationship: When you're giving each other "brojobs."

DRUGSTORE COW

New Rule: Stop pretending your drugs are morally superior to my drugs because you get yours at a store. This week, they released the autopsy report on Anna Nicole Smith, and the cause of death was what I always thought it was: mad cow. No, it turns out she had nine different prescription drugs in her—which, in the medical field, is known as the "full Limbaugh." They opened her up, and a Walgreens jumped out. Antidepressants, anti-anxiety pills, sleeping pills, sedatives, Valium, methadone—this woman was killed by her doctor, who is a glorified bartender. I'm not going to say his name, but only because (a) I don't want to get sued, and (b) my back is killing me.

This month marks the thirty-fifth anniversary of a famous government report. I was sixteen in 1972, and I remember how excited we were when Nixon's much ballyhooed National Commission on Drug Abuse came out and said pot should be legalized. It was a moment of great hope for common sense—and then, just like Bush did with the Iraq Study Group, Nixon took the report and threw it in the garbage, and from there the '70s went right into disco and colored underpants.

This week in *American Scientist,* a magazine George Bush wouldn't read if he got food poisoning in Mexico and it was the only thing he could reach from the toilet, described a study done in England that measured the lethality of various drugs, and found tobacco and alcohol far worse than pot, LSD, or Ecstasy—which pretty much mirrors my own experiments in this same area. The Beatles took LSD and wrote *Sgt. Pepper*—Anna Nicole Smith took legal drugs and couldn't remember the number for nine-one-one.

I wish I had more time to go into the fact that the drug war has always been about keeping black men from voting by finding out what they're addicted to and making it illegal—it's a miracle our government hasn't outlawed fat white women yet—but I leave with one request: Would someone please just make a bumper sticker that says, "I'm a stoner, and I vote."

—*March 30, 2007*

E

CTRL+ALT+ELITE

New Rule: Now that liberals have taken back the word "liberal," they also have to take back the word "elite." By now you've heard the constant right-wing attacks on the "elite media," and the "liberal elite." Who may or may not be part of the "Washington elite." A subset of the "East Coast elite." Which is overly influenced by the "Hollywood elite." So basically, unless you're a shit-kicker from Kansas, you're with the terrorists. If you played a drinking game where you did a shot every time Rush Limbaugh attacked someone for being "elite," you'd be almost as wasted as Rush Limbaugh.

I don't get it: In other fields—outside of government—elite is a good thing, like an elite fighting force. Tiger Woods is an elite golfer. If I need brain surgery, I'd like an elite doctor. But in politics, elite is bad—the elite aren't down-to-earth and accessible like you and me and President Shit-for-Brains.

Which is fine, except that whenever there's a Bush administration scandal, it always traces back to some incompetent political hack appointment, and you think to yourself, "Where are they getting these screwups from?" Well, now we know: from Pat Robertson. I'm not kidding. Take Monica Goodling, who before she resigned last week because she's smack in the middle of the U.S. attorneys scandal, was the third-ranking official in the Justice Department of the United States. She's thirty-three, and though she never even worked as a prosecutor, was tasked with overseeing the job performance of all ninety-three U.S. attorneys. How do you get to the top that fast? Harvard? Princeton? No, Goodling did her undergraduate work at Messiah College—you know, home of the "Fighting Christies"—and then went on to attend Pat Robertson's law school.

Yes, Pat Robertson, the man who said the presence of gay people at Disney World would cause "earthquakes, tornadoes, and possibly a meteor," has a law school. And what kid wouldn't want to attend? It's three years, and you have to read only one book. *U.S. News & World Report,* which does the definitive ranking of colleges, lists Regent as a tier-four school, which is the lowest score it gives. It's not a hard school to get into. You have to renounce Satan and draw a pirate on a matchbook. This is for the people who couldn't get into the University of Phoenix.

Now, would you care to guess how many graduates of this televangelist diploma mill work in the Bush administration? One hundred fifty. And you wonder why things are so messed up? We're talking about a top Justice Department official who went to a college founded by a TV host. Would you send your daughter to Maury Povich U? And if you did, would you expect her to get a job at the White House? In two hundred years, we've gone from "we the people" to "up with people." From the best and brightest to dumb and dumber. And where better to find people dumb enough to believe in George Bush than Pat Robertson's law school? The problem here in America isn't that the country is being run by elites. It's that it's being run by a bunch of hayseeds. And by the way, the lawyer Monica Goodling hired to keep her ass out of jail went to a real law school.

—April 13, 2007

EAU DE HUMANITY

New Rule: Celebrity colognes must actually smell like the celebrity. Tim McGraw's new cologne is, quote, "a lush combination of lavender, amber, patchouli, and sandalwood." While the actual Tim McGraw is a spicy combination of beef jerky, Pabst Blue Ribbon, and WD-40. And make way for the newest celebrity cologne: McCain . . .

. . . with its alluring combination of flop sweat, creamed corn, and Preparation H.

ENOUGH ALMIGHTY

New Rule: Since in a recent poll only fifteen percent of Americans said they believe in evolution, America must change its name to the United States of Jesus Christ. And our motto from *"E Pluribus Unum"* to "I'm with Stupid." The good news for the nation? If we get any stupider about science, we'll forget how to cook crystal meth.

EXXXON

New Rule: If I'm paying four bucks a gallon for gas, that TV in the pump has to show porn. This way, I'm not the only one at the pump taking it in the ass.

BIO-DEBATABLE

New Rule: From now on, Earth Day really must be a year-round thing. And in honor of this Earth Day, starting Monday, supermarket clerks must stop putting the big bottle of detergent with a handle on it in a plastic bag. I don't mean to tell you how to do your job, but you see that handle you just lifted the detergent with? I can use that *same* handle to carry the detergent to my car. And stop putting my liquor in a smaller paper sack before you put it in the big paper sack with my other stuff. What, are you afraid my groceries will think less of me if they see I've been drinking? Trust me, the broccoli doesn't care, and the condoms already know.

Here's a quote from Albert Einstein: "If the bee disappeared off the surface of the globe, then man would have only four years of life left. No more bees, no more pollination, no more plants, no more animals, no more man." Well, guess what? The bees are disappearing. In massive numbers. All around the world. And if you think I'm being alarmist and that "Oh, they'll figure out some way to pollinate the plants . . ." No, they've tried. For a lot of what we eat, only bees work. And they're not working. They're gone. It's called colony collapse disorder, when the hive's inhabitants suddenly disappear, and all that's left are a few queens and some immature workers—like when a party winds down at Elton John's house.

But I think we're the ones suffering from colony collapse disorder. Because although nobody really knows for sure what's killing the bees, it's not Al Qaeda, and it's not God doing some of his Old Testament shtick, and it's not Winnie-the-Pooh. It's us. It could be from pesticides, or genetically modified food, or global warming, or the high-fructose corn syrup we started to feed them. Recently, it was discovered that bees won't fly near cell phones—the electromagnetic signals they emit might screw up the bees' navigation system, knocking them out of the sky. So thanks, bigmouth in line at Starbucks, you just killed us. It's nature's way of saying, "Can you hear me now?"

Recently I asked: If it solved global warming, would you give up the TV remote and go back to carting your ass over to the television set every time you wanted to change the channel? If it comes down to the cell phone vs. the bee, will we choose to literally blather ourselves to death?

Will we continue to tell ourselves that we don't have to solve environmental problems—we can just adapt: build seawalls instead of stopping the ice caps from melting. Don't save the creatures of the earth and oceans, just learn to eat the slime and jellyfish that nothing can kill, like Chinese restaurants are already doing.

Maybe you don't need to talk on your cell phone all the time. Maybe you don't need a bag when you buy a keychain. Americans throw out one hundred billion plastic bags a year, and they all take a thousand years to decompose. Your children's children's children will never know you, but they'll know you once bought batteries at the 99 cent store, because the bag will still be caught in a tree. Except there won't be any trees. Please educate someone about the birds and the bees, because without bees, humans become the canary in the coal mine, and we make bad canaries, because we're already such sheep.

—April 20, 2007

F

FRENCH DISSING

New Rule: Conservatives have to stop rolling their eyes every time they hear the word "France." Like just calling something French is the ultimate argument winner. As if to say, "What can you say about a country that was too stupid to get on board with our wonderfully conceived and brilliantly executed war in Iraq?" And yet an American politician could not survive if he uttered the simple, true statement "France has a better health-care system than we do, and we should steal it." Because here, simply dismissing an idea as French passes for an argument. John Kerry? Couldn't vote for him—he looked French. Yeah, as opposed to the other guy, who just looked stupid.

Last week, France had an election, and people over there approach an election differently. They vote. Eighty-five percent turned out. You couldn't get eighty-five percent of Americans to get off the couch if there was an election between tits and bigger tits and they were giving out free samples.

Maybe the high turnout has something to do with the fact that the French candidates are never asked where they stand on evolution, prayer in school, abortion, stem cell research, or gay marriage. And if the candidate knows about a character in a book other than Jesus, it's not a drawback. The electorate doesn't vote for the guy they want to have a croissant with. Nor do they care about private lives: In the current race, Madame Royal has four kids, but she never got married. And she's a socialist. In America, if a Democrat even thinks you're calling him "liberal," he grabs an orange vest and a rifle and heads into the woods to kill something.

Royal's opponent *is* married, but they live apart and lead separate lives. And the people are *okay* with that, for the same reason they're okay with nude beaches: because they're not a nation of six-year-olds who scream and giggle if they see pee-pee parts. They have weird ideas about privacy. They think it should be private. In France, even mistresses have mistresses. To not have a lady on the side says to the voters, "I'm no good at multitasking."

Like any country, France has its faults, like all that ridiculous accordion music—but their health care is the best in the industrialized world, as is their poverty rate. And they're completely independent of Mid-East oil. And they're the greenest country. And they're not fat. They have public intellectuals in France. We have Dr. Phil. They invented sex during the day, lingerie, and the tongue. Can't we admit we could learn *something* from them?

—*May 4, 2007*

FACE OFF

New Rule: Stop showing me pictures of celebrities I used to think were hot without makeup. If Christina Aguilera wanted us to see what she looks like first thing in the morning, she'd pass out faceup.

FAILURE TO LUNCH

New Rule: If you work in an office, you have to take a turn cleaning the office microwave. I opened ours the other day and a bat flew out. The inside looks like a Jackson Pollock painting. The three settings are now "cook," "defrost," and "hepatitis." If you're not going to clean the damn thing, at least take out whatever is growing in there so we can harvest the stem cells.

FAITH HEEL

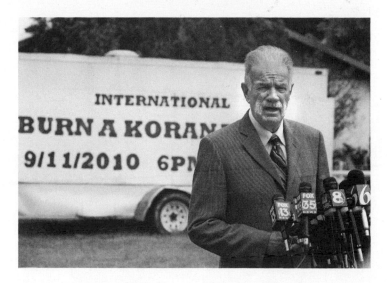

New Rule: In the future, you don't need to show us the picture of guys like Terry Jones. Once you tell us he's an Evangelical pastor, he's from Florida, and he wants to burn the Koran to send a message to them A-rabs . . . we're pretty sure he looks like this.

FASHION OF THE CHRIST

New Rule: If you're known for beating the mother of your child, you probably shouldn't wear a wife-beater.

FASHION STATEMENT

New Rule: The president of Iran needs a makeover. You're a nuclear power now; isn't it time you dressed like it? You've got 160 centrifuges—and one suit. Forget enriching uranium, you need to enrich your wardrobe. You're going to wipe Israel off the face of the earth looking like *that*? I don't think so. You're on Schindler's Worst-Dressed List.

FEMINOSEY

New Rule: Stop trying to "fix" men. Scientists have developed a hormone-laced nasal spray that makes men more emotional and sensitive. It's called Gaysonex. And the only side effects are dry mouth, a mild headache, and a slight tingling around your vagina. Ladies, what if we developed a drug that made you more horny and easy? I mean, besides vodka and Red Bull.

FENDER NEUTRAL

MY CHILD IS AN
HONOR STUDENT
AT WOODBURY MIDDLE SCHOOL

New Rule: Schools need bumper stickers for the kids who are *never* going to be honor students. Why punish the low achievers? How about bumper stickers that say . . .

FINGER BANG

New Rule: Stop criticizing the company that distributes Braille porn. Why shouldn't the sightless enjoy porn? What, are they gonna go *more* blind?

FIRTH CONTROL

New Rule: Colin Firth has to admit that he's not a human being but a robot designed by women as the perfect man. He's handsome, charming, witty, he's got that accent and a gay best friend . . . the only way he could be any better is if he ejaculated Häagen-Dazs.

FIRTH PRIZE

New Rule: If they're going to make a historical epic, full of British actors, in period costumes, about Queen Elizabeth helping her father get over his speech impediment, why bother having the Oscars at all? You win. Unless someone in America is making a movie where Meryl Streep teaches Anne Frank to box, we give up.

FIZZ ED

New Rule: Guys, you don't need *both* Ed Hardy fashions *and* Ed Hardy booze. Either one alone is enough to make Snooki do you in the men's room.

FIZZLE STICK

New Rule: Sorry, North Korea, it's not an "intercontinental ballistic missile" unless it can get all the way to another continent. If all you ever hit is the ocean, what you've got is a torpedo.

FLICK OR TREAT

New Rule: Your list of scary movies to watch on Halloween has to include scary movies. *The Birds* isn't scary. It's ridiculous. *The Blair Witch Project*? That's two hours of watching people get lost in the woods, followed by motion sickness. You want to see a real scary movie? Try *Jesus Camp*.

FLIGHT RISK

New Rule: Jesus is not my copilot. The CEO of Ryanair says he wants to cut costs by eliminating the copilot. And if something happens to the pilot, having a flight attendant land the plane. Unless she's reading her Dean Koontz novel. In which case the plane will be flown remotely by some guy named Sanjay in Bangalore. Which is all fine. As long as they change their motto to "Ryanair—We Dare You."

FOLK YOU

New Rule: The only thing worse than Christmas music is Christmas music sung by Bob Dylan. Presenting *Christmas in the Heart,* holiday favorites as only an elderly, tone-deaf Jew can sing them. Years ago, Bob's people killed Jesus; now they're murdering his music. The good news: The profits go to charity. The bad news: The charity isn't the Bob Dylan Vocal Cord Transplant Foundation.

FOR BEAT'S SAKE

New Rule: You can't call it house music if no one has ever played it in their house. Call it what it really is, "so shitty you have to take a drug called Ecstasy just to make it bearable" music. We had this when I was a kid—it was called "the record is skipping."

FORMAL COMPLAINT

New Rule: You can't tell me you're making James Bond up-to-date when he's still wearing a tuxedo to the casino. Have you even been to Laughlin, Nevada? You're lucky if the player sitting next to you puts his teeth in. You know how you can tell a high roller? His sweatpants are clean. There's a name for people who wear tuxedos in casinos: magicians.

FUEL ME ONCE . . .

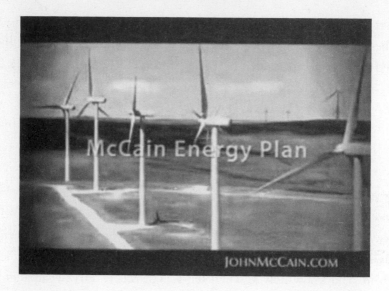

New Rule: You can't put a windmill in your campaign ad if you voted against every single bill that might lead to someone building one. As long as you're sending a camera crew to a farm, why not just take a picture of actual bullshit?

HEAVEN CAN HATE

New Rule: Death isn't always sad. This week, the Reverend Jerry Falwell died, and millions of Americans asked, "Why? Why, God? Why . . . didn't you take Pat Robertson with him?" I don't want to say Jerry was disliked by the gay community, but tonight in New York City, at exactly eight o'clock, Broadway theaters along the Great White Way turned their lights up for two minutes.

I know you're not supposed to speak ill of the dead, but I think we can make an exception, because speaking ill of the dead was kind of Jerry Falwell's hobby. He's the guy who said AIDS was God's punishment for homosexuality and that 9/11 was brought on by pagans, abortionists, feminists, gays, and the ACLU—or, as I like to call them, my studio audience.

It was surreal watching people on the news praise Falwell, followed by a clip package of what he actually said—things like:

"Homosexuals are part of a vile and satanic system that will be utterly annihilated." "If you're not a born-again Christian, you're a failure as a human being." "Feminists just need a man in the house." "There is no separation of church and state." And, of course, everyone's favorite: "The purple Teletubby is gay."

Jerry Falwell found out you could launder your hate through the cover of "God's will"—he didn't hate gays, God does.

All Falwell's power came from name-dropping God, and gay people should steal that trick. Don't say you want something because it's your right as a human being—say you want it because it's your religion.

Gay men have been going at things backward. Forget civil rights, and just make gayness a religion. I mean, you're kneeling anyway. And it's easy to start a religion. Watch, I'll do it for you.

I had a vision last night. The Blessed Virgin Mary came to me—I don't know how she got past the guards—and she told me it's time to take the high ground from the Seventh-day Adventists and give it to the twenty-four-hour party people. And that what happens in the confessional stays in the confessional. Gay men, don't say you're life partners. Say you're a nunnery of two. "We weren't having sex, officer. I was performing a very private mass. Here in my car. I was letting my rod and my staff comfort him."

One can only hope that as Jerry Falwell now approaches the pearly gates, he is met there by God Himself, wearing a Fire Island muscle shirt and nut-hugger shorts, and saying to Jerry in a mighty lisp, "I'm not talking to you."

—*May 18, 2007*

G

GAG ORDER

New Rule: Some celebrity needs to raise awareness about the dangers of autoerotic asphyxiation. Yes, we've lost another talent to jerking yourself purple while choking yourself blue, this time the host of a British TV show. So come on, Hollywood, where's the telethon? We are the world. We are the children. We are the ones who make a brighter day, so let's stop masturbating with a noose around our necks.

GAG RULE

New Rule: There aren't 101 sex tricks. In fact, ladies, there's only one—it's called a blowjob. Do it 101 times.

GATEWAY DRUG

New Rule: Stop putting psychedelic screensavers on computers. I sit down to check my e-mail, and the next thing I know it's three days later, I'm in the desert, I'm banging on a drum, I'm naked, and somebody's pierced my dick.

GERM LIMITS

New Rule: Don't put that in your mouth. A new study finds that dangerous drug-resistant staph infections in children have increased tenfold over the past decade. And for you little ones out there, the infection eats you alive, and then you never see Mommy and Daddy again. And you get it from being on a plane and kicking the back of my seat.

RED POISONING

New Rule: If you were surprised that the Chinese don't care about toy safety, the child who needs protecting is you. Over the last couple of months, American consumers have been learning a shocking lesson about supply and demand: If you demand products that don't cost anything, people will make them out of poison, mud, and shit.

Since April, approximately seventeen million toys in the United States, all of them made in China, have been recalled. Which is amazing, considering that no one in the Department of Justice can recall a thing. Now, believe me, I was devastated when Mattel recalled almost everything in my Barbie Dream Closet, although I had suspected something when Ken discovered a lump on his testicle.

Until recently, I never worried about being harmed by the Chinese, unless they were in the left-hand turn lane. But then we found out that their dog food was deadly and they were making toothpaste out of antifreeze. And that the number 62A over at the Szechwan Palace is beef with bronchitis. They don't care if your precious little Britney sucks a little lead. Because in China, their kids aren't playing with the toys. They're the ones in the factory all day making them.

Now, I know you're saying, "But, Bill, I don't have time to ponder whether these $12 jeans are the product of child labor. I just know I'm an American on a budget, and our lifestyle is a blessed one, and I want to look nice while standing in line for my iPhone."

But there is something to be said for thinking about why these bargains are such bargains. Walmart is the most American thing in the universe, but all it sells is crap from China. Walmart wouldn't exist without the American consumers' endless thirst for the cheapest stuff China has to offer, like $30 DVD players and Jackie Chan.

In America, there is nothing more sacred than a bargain, and that even includes the war. There's too much lead in the kids' toys but not nearly enough on the Humvees in Iraq.

Let's have a war and cut taxes! What could go wrong? Let's give mortgages to the homeless! Sounds like a plan! Let's buy toys from a communist police state. You just know they'll put in a little extra love. Speaking of which, do you know why today's modern Chinese capitalist puts lead in the paint that goes on toys? Because it makes colors brighter. You gotta love America: a country that's literally being killed by the stuff that makes objects shiny.

—August 24, 2007

G.I. FAUX

New Rule: Marine recruiting ads have to stop it with the rock climbing and dragon slaying. I'm no stickler for truth in advertising, but this is like marketing Doritos as a douche. What's wrong with advertising what Marines really do? They get to protect America, shoot bad people legally, and serve as the advance team for Halliburton.

GLENN SCARY GLENN LOST

New Rule: Since Glenn Beck is clearly onto us, liberals must launch our plan for socialist domination immediately. Listen closely, comrades. I've received word from General Soros and our partners in the UN—Operation Streisand is a go. Markos Moulitsas, you and your *Daily Kos*–controlled army of gay Mexican day laborers will join with Michael Moore's Prius tank division north of Branson, where you will seize the guns of everyone who doesn't blame America first, forcing them into the FEMA concentration camps. That's where ACORN and I will re-educate them as atheists and declare victory in the War on Christmas.

GOD 'N' PLENTY

New Rule: If an Evangelical tries to use Halloween to pimp Jesus to kids, they get to egg his house. On Halloween, the president of the American Family Association urged his flock to hand out a Christian-based comic book instead of candy. Excuse me, Halloween isn't a time to push your beliefs. You don't see me handing out pot to kids . . . Okay, well not the little kids.

GOD SAVE THE TWEEN

New Rule: The boys' room at Chuck E. Cheese's must install a condom machine. A thirteen-year-old in the UK just became a father, bringing a whole new meaning to the phrase "baby daddy." You know you're too young to be a dad when your excuse for not getting up for the midnight feeding is "monsters under my bed."

GORY HOLE

New Rule: The White House doesn't have to release the dead Bin Laden photos, but don't pretend we can't take it. We've seen pictures of Britney Spears's vagina getting out of a car. Television has desensitized us to violence, and porn has desensitized us to people getting shot in the eye.

THE GRAPE ESCAPE

New Rule: The Napa Valley is Disneyland for alcoholics. Be honest, you're not visiting twenty wineries in four days because you're an oenophile, you're doing it because you're a drunk. It's the only place in America where you can pass out in a stranger's house and it's okay, because it's a B&B and you paid for it.

GRECIAN, EARN

New Rule: President Obama must not bail out Greece. Besides democracy, philosophy, geometry, poetry, architecture, and drama, what have they ever given us? Greek president George Papandreau came to Washington, begging for money. To which I say: Screw you, Zorba, and the horse you came hidden inside of. You want our hard-earned tax dollars? Come back when you're an insurance company.

GRIDDLE ME THIS

New Rule: Stop lying to me about your pancake mix. The back of the box says 1½ cups makes ten to twelve pancakes. Really? 'Cause I get four. Who's your cook, Jesus?

GROSS DOMESTIC PRODUCT

New Rule: 7-Eleven doesn't need its own brand. I don't come into 7-Eleven because of the allure of the name. I come into 7-Eleven to steal rolling papers while the clerk's stocking the cooler. Here's a marketing tip, 7-Eleven: Take that time you put into product development and clean the microwave.

GYM CARRY

New Rule: Joggers have to leave the Batman utility belt at home. You've got two water bottles, a protein shake, an iPod, an odometer, headphones, car keys, pepper spray, and some gizmo that uploads your heart rate onto your Twitter page. Meanwhile, those German women who win every marathon can run thirty miles uphill drinking only the sweat that drips from their mustaches.

PHARMERS MARKET

New Rule: If you believe you need to take all the pills the pharmaceutical industry says you do, then you're already on drugs. Yes, it's that time in the campaign where all the candidates are presenting their health-care proposals. But none of the plans address the real problem: We won't stop being sick until we stop making ourselves sick.

Because there is a point where even the most universal government health program can't help you. They can't outlaw unhealthy food or alcohol or cigarettes. Just pot, sadly. The government isn't your nanny. They're your dealer. And they subsidize illness in America. They have to; there's too much money in it. There's no money in healthy people. And there's no money in dead people. The money is in the middle—people who are alive, sort of, but with one or more chronic conditions that put them in need of Celebrex or Nasonex or Valtrex or Lunesta.

Fifty years ago, children didn't even get type 2 diabetes. Now it's an emerging epidemic, as are a long list of ailments that used to be rare and now have been mainstreamed—things like asthma and autism and acid reflux . . . arthritis, allergies, adult acne, attention deficit disorder—and that's just the A's.

Doesn't anyone wonder why we live with all this illness? I'll tell you why: At the L.A. County Fair, they were serving something called "fried Coke." My first thought was, "Gosh, what a waste of a perfectly good eight ball." But no. They actually pour the Coca-Cola syrup into the deep fryer, then put it in a cup, and top it with sugar and whipped cream, and a cherry—you know, because fruit is good for you. Would it really be that much more unhealthy to get molested by one of the carnies?

In Hillary Clinton's health plan, the words "nutrition" and "exercise" appeared once. The word "drugs"? *Fourteen* times. Just as the pharmaceutical companies want it. Their ad weasels love to say, "When diet and exercise fail . . ." Well, diet and exercise *don't* fail, a fact brought home by a new Duke University study that showed exercise—yes, exercise—to be just as effective a cure for depression as Paxil and Zoloft. So, *ask* your doctor if Getting Off *Your* Ass is right for you.

—September 28, 2007

H

HAIL BARRY

New Rule: It's okay for the president to play ball in the house. It's easy to judge and say this scene detracts from the dignity of the White House—until you consider the end zone is between Clinton's semen stain and where Bush OD'd on a pretzel.

HAIRPORT

New Rule: There are worse things on airplanes than terrorists. Virgin Airlines is promoting the power outlets on their planes with this ad of a woman blow-drying her hair at thirty thousand feet. After washing it in what, the blue liquid in the toilet? Air travel is bad enough without turning it into a flying locker room. "Let's see, twenty minutes before landing, I've got just enough time to shave my balls."

HAIR'S JONNY!

New Rule: There's just something about a crew cut that says, "You can trust me." This is Montana Senator Jon Tester. I don't know much about him, and I don't need to. His hair says it all: "I'm friendly. . . . I'm dependable. . . . I'm *literally* levelheaded." If hair could smile, it would look like this. And most important, it's hair that says, "You will never, ever find me snorting meth with a gay hooker."

HAMPER PROOF

New Rule: If the doctor makes you take off your clothes, he has to provide somewhere to put your clothes. It's bad enough I have to sit in this cold exam room wearing a paper dress; I also have to cradle all my clothes in my arms like I'm boarding the train to Auschwitz. You've got a million dollars' worth of equipment in there, Doc—how about a hook on the wall. Yes, I could pile my clothes on top of the hazardous-waste container, or the table where dozens of men get their prostate exams every day, but on second thought . . . I'll just hold them.

LEVI ON A JET PLANE

New Rule: If we can't, after all is said and done, make this election go the right way, at least we can save one man. I'm talking about young Master Levi Johnston. He's the eighteen-year-old Alaskan hockey enthusiast who knocked up Sarah Palin's daughter, and the *National Enquirer* describes him as "a boozing pot-smoker who doesn't want to get married"— and John McCain thinks he found *his* soul mate!

We've all seen how evil henchmen of the Republican party captured this poor innocent out of his natural habitat and forced him into a shotgun engagement because when the seventeen-year-old daughter of the vice presidential candidate is "out to here," it's just better that Levi was introduced as the "fiancé." Looks a little less white-trashy.

But that doesn't change the fact that Levi is America's number-one political prisoner. But, Levi, you don't have to be—this is the twenty-first century, at least in the blue states. You don't have to do this—you have options. You can pull a *Juno*—fuck, you live in Juneau! Or you could do what most people do with an unwanted child: Give it to Angelina Jolie.

And if you're worried about the baby, don't. Let's get real, dude, the way you are at eighteen, a baby's better off not being around you—you'll wind up losing it, or shooting it, or it'll be on the bottom of your skate or something. Just let the Palin womenfolk look after it for a while. One more infant in that Mormon compound they call a house won't bother anybody—they'll barely notice another kid at the table, and soon they won't even remember whose seed it was that produced young Trink or Truck or Puck, or whatever fucked-up redneck name they give him.

In any event, we here at *Real Time* have taken the liberty of purchasing the website FreeLevi.org. It's yours if you want to use it to get folks to contribute to some sort of liberty fund so you can get enough money to get out of that frozen meth lab they call a town. And even if the money doesn't come in, it's not too late: Just grab your skull bong, climb out the window, and get on the highway. I can't actually come get you, or even let you stay at my place, because I'm pretty sure you'd smoke all my weed, but just call me from a pay phone, I know of a safe house you can stay in till after the election; it's like the witness protection program for baby daddies.

And remember, Levi: California knows how to party. Trust me, the girls out here are going to love a big, high-sticking farm boy like you. If you play your cards right, in a couple weeks you could be screwing the lesbian right out of Lindsay Lohan.

—September 19, 2008

HANNIBAL LECTURE

New Rule: Stop making horror movies with Anthony Hopkins. I'm not afraid of any evil I can evade by taking the stairs two at a time. Anthony Hopkins was a great young Shakespearean actor. Just ask Shakespeare. But if I wanted a movie where an eighty-year-old made my blood run cold, I'd rent *Sex and the City II*.

HARD RIGHT

New Rule: The next Republican National Convention must be held in a giant closet. Every week there's a new gay Republican outed. I have a feeling that "big tent" they're always talking about is in their pants. There are so many Republicans in the closet, their symbol shouldn't be an elephant, it should be a moth.

HARDLY MERKIN

New Rule: Bring back a little pubic hair. Not a lot, I'm not talking about reviving that 1973 look that said "I'm liberated" and "I'm smuggling a hedgehog." I just want a friendly, fuzzy calling card that's a middle ground between toddler smooth and "Dr. Livingston, I presume?" It's supposed to have *some* hair on it. It's a pussy, not Dr. Evil's cat. Call me old school, but there's a name for a guy who needs it hair-free: He's called a pedophile.

HATE-BY-TEN

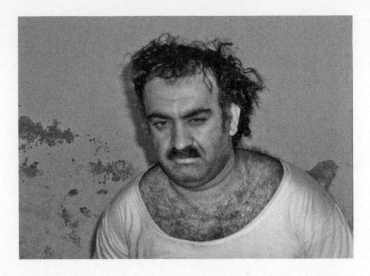

New Rule: Khalid Sheikh Mohammed must get a new head shot. I don't care how long your résumé is, with this photo you'll be lucky to get a gig blowing up a dinner theater. Look at you. You're like the Arab Nick Nolte. You look like Ron Jeremy with a hangover. You think you were tortured before—wait until we start waxing off all that chest hair. And by the way, Sheikh, there's nothing chic about that outfit. That shirt doesn't say, "Death to America," it says, "*Flashdance*: What a Feeling!" I can't believe we have the same agent.

HELL SINKY

New Rule: Restaurant restroom sinks must not be so trendy that I can't figure out how to turn them on. Do I wave my hand in front of an electronic eye? Is it voice-activated? Does it scan my retina? I know these sinks are supposed to be the state of the art in hygiene, but the guy next to me is peeing in his.

HEMLINE NEWS

New Rule: If one of your news organization's headlines is about who got kicked off *Dancing with the Stars* last night, you're no longer a news organization. Sort of like, if you were on *Dancing with the Stars* last night, you're no longer a star.

HESS WE CAN

New Rule: Stop talking about "the gas prices under Obama." As if he's the guy out there changing the numbers on the sign with that long pole. And while they're at the gas station, Republicans who still think human activity doesn't affect air quality should poke their heads in the men's room.

HIGH FINANCE

New Rule: Stop acting so surprised that ninety percent of our paper money has cocaine on it. This is America. You're lucky it doesn't have gravy on it. Besides, if it weren't for the coke, a dollar wouldn't have any value at all.

HILLBILLY HEROINE

New Rule: If you're a baby momma trying to hide your baby daddy's baby behind your momma's baby . . . you just might be a redneck. At least when Obama got a convention bump, it wasn't leaking amniotic fluid.

HITTING BOTTOM

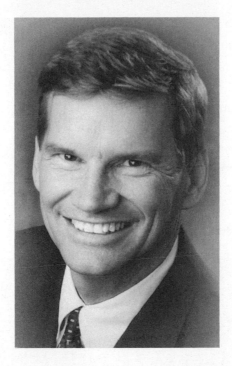

New Rule: You can't make a gay man one hundred percent straight in less than a month. Especially if that month contains Fashion Week. A month to change your sexuality? I've spent longer than that on hold trying to quit AOL. Guys like Ted Haggard can't just claim to be "cured" of homosexuality; they should be forced to blow into some sort of "Dicka-lyzer."

HOARDER PATROL

New Rule: Someone has to make a reality show about hoarders who hoard midgets. I'm too busy to watch all the shows about hoarders and all the shows about midgets. So put them together. I'm also too busy for shows about sexual predators and shows about cake. So put those together, too. Make a show about sexual predators who hoard midgets after they lure them into their homes with cake.

HOLY SEE-THROUGH

New Rule: The Pope must wear a slip. I'm sorry, but some people just shouldn't do "casual Friday." And I don't understand, usually the Catholic Church is so good about covering things up.

HOT TOTTY

New Rule: Women have to stop using baby pictures in their Facebook profiles. Especially if it's your daughter as a baby. You've taken something nice—your old high school boyfriend looking you up on Facebook to masturbate—and turned it into something creepy.

HULLS OF MONTEZUMA

New Rule: A cruise ship to Mexico is newsworthy only if everyone doesn't get diarrhea. "In the morning, in the evening, ain't we got the runs . . ." You want the Mexican cruise experience? Let me save you six grand. Put on Univision and eat at Wendy's.

EBONY AND IRONY

New Rule: A candidate for president should not be judged by the color of his skin. To anyone who thinks like this, I say: Please don't reject John McCain just because he's white. I think the recent news from Wall Street has made us all less tolerant and only reinforced the stereotype that white people are shiftless, thieving welfare queens.

Take a look at the CEOs of Fannie Mae, Freddie Mac, AIG, and Lehman Brothers. I know—the first thing that jumps out at you about their faces is that they all happen to be white, and they all happen to be responsible for stealing. But what you have to understand is that these whites are a product of a society that made them that way. It was the neighborhoods, and the schools they went to—Harvard, Yale, the Wharton School of Business. They never learned the value of doing real, actual work. And the first step in fixing that is better role models, so kids growing up white today don't think the only way out of Westchester is corporate crime, or a government handout, or sailing.

So I get it, the temptation is to look at McCain and vote against him because you don't see an individual; you see just another typical "welfare whitey."

And it's true, he's spent his entire life shuffling from one low-paying government job to another. Well, except for those years he spent in prison. Typical! And between you and me, he's not very articulate. Oh, he may have some "street smarts," but he's not what you'd call an educated man. He freely admits that he's ignorant about the economy, and apparently the only thing his white running mate knows how to do is crank out one baby after another. And now, of course, her teenage daughter is pregnant out of wedlock, because she learns it at home! But that doesn't mean we should assume all white people are like that just because so many of them are.

There is hope. I believe even the stupidest, greediest, laziest whites can break the cycle of dependence, like this November, when we finally move George Bush out of public housing.

—*September 26, 2008*

THE HURL OF SANDWICH

New Rule: Bacon, eggs, and cheese between two waffles isn't a breakfast; it's a suicide attempt. This is Dunkin' Donuts' new "waffle sandwich." You can wait in line for yours or, if you're in a hurry, just snatch the pistol from the cop sitting at the counter and shoot yourself in the head.

HURLIN' OLSEN

New Rule: If you lose your looks at fifteen, you're doing something wrong. I've seen less frightening twins in *The Shining*. Steven Tyler saw this and said, "Wait. There are two of me, and I'm on the cover of *Newsweek*? Who did my makeup? I look like shit."

HYPE CASTING

New Rule: Now that all news on CNN and Fox News, no matter how old, is being billed as "breaking news" or "happening now," news that *actually is* breaking and/or happening now must get its own graphic that says, "No, seriously, guys, we're not fucking around this time, this is actually happening now."

I SHOT THE SERIF

New Rule: The Gap doesn't need a new logo. It needs to stop being the place with the expensive cheap clothes that asks the question, "How can something without any style still go out of style?" Remember, none of us are in the Gap because of the logo. Or because of the clerk who says, "Those jeans look cute on you." We're all in here for one reason and one reason only: because some old person, who doesn't know any better, got us a gift card.

ICE RACK

New Rule: Men don't care how expensive your bra is; they just need to know if it unfastens in the front or the back. The Victoria's Secret Christmas catalog features a $6.5 million diamond-studded bra. And guys, it's the perfect bra for mistresses, because she's almost guaranteed not to leave it in your truck.

IDIOM SAVANT

New Rule: Instead of using the expression "It is what it is," just shut up.

IMMACULATE REJECTION

New Rule: For the sake of human existence, K-Fed must not be allowed to mate with Paris Hilton. Or, as I like to call her, "K-Y." When the Pope saw this picture, he changed his opinion on abortion from "It's murder" to "Okay, but just this once."

IMMODEST PROPOSAL

New Rule: No more public marriage proposals. When you hire a sky-writing plane, or propose to your girlfriend at the ball game, every un-married woman is looking at her man like, "Well . . . ?" And you're not helping the married men, either, whose wives are remembering how they proposed to them in flip-flops, cargo shorts, and a "Who Farted?" T-shirt by saying, "What the hell, I'm going bald anyway."

POTUS ENVY

New Rule: The rest of the world can go back to being completely jealous of America. Our majority-white country just freely elected a black president, something no other democracy has ever done. Take that, Canada. Where's your Nubian warrior president? Your head of state is a boring white dude named *Stephen Harper,* and mine is a kick-ass black ninja named *Barack Hussein Obama.*

That's right, everybody, I take back every bad thing I ever said about the good old USA. I've gone from "God damn America" to "Goddamn, America!" I feel like a hockey mom at the state fair getting felt up by Hank Williams Jr. while fireworks go off and Jesus appears in my cotton candy. It would be stupid not to be stupid about it. So I'd like to take this moment, when we finally got one right, to bask in a little unwarranted, unapologetic, irrational faux patriotism. Or, as Fox News calls it, "regular programming."

I might regret this. It's kinda like grocery shopping when you're high. But here goes, world: We're Americans. We built the Golden Gate Bridge, the Hoover Dam, and Joan Rivers. We're the only country that can look at a sandwich made of ice cream and chocolate cookies covered in fudge and think, "Hmm, you think we could fry that?" And you know what? Yes, we can! They may have seventy-two virgins, but we have thirty-one flavors. You know what our favorite burger topping is? Another burger. We invented rock 'n' roll, jazz, funk, R&B, and hip-hop. Without our music, your iPods would be filled with ABBA, Menudo, and Men at Work. And you wouldn't have iPods.

Not only did we create the Internet, we're the ones who filled it up with porn. Jefferson lived here. And Miles Davis. And Gloria Steinem and Frank Lloyd Wright. And a lot of other people Sarah Palin never heard of. In America, strippers and Disney stars have an equal right to be named Hannah Montana, and I was freely able to make a movie saying there's no afterlife, and you could watch it while eating crap that'll kill you. But that's okay, because our corn-fed high school sophomores are bigger than your soldiers. And they're better armed.

I ask you, in what other nation would they tax young people to make sure old people can afford erections? What you call "football," we call "soccer." And what you call "war crimes," we call "football." And let me just say it again: We elected a black guy, and it was because he was the best candidate, not because it was some cheap gimmick. And we should know, because we are also the country that invented cheap gimmicks! Yes, America is like Jessica Simpson—sometimes it's so stupid it embarrasses you, but on the other hand, how about them titties?

—November 14, 2008

INCENSED

New Rule: You're not allowed to be shocked that breathing smoke might be bad for you. A new study shows that frequently burning incense might cause cancer. What—did you think you were protected by some kind of magic hippie force field? It comes down to what I always say—if you're going to burn something and then inhale it, it might as well be getting you high.

INDIAN CAREGIVER

New Rule: Give America back to the Indians. In reaction to the South Dakota abortion ban, the Oglala Sioux Indian tribe plans to open an abortion clinic on their sovereign lands in the state. Oooh, red man gives paleface heap big screw you! Now women in South Dakota will have an alternative to throwing themselves off a grain elevator. Just look for the teepee with the sign that says, "Papoose? Vamoose!"

INFERIOR COMPLEX

New Rule: If Mormons are going to keep putting up temples, their architecture has to suck less. Gee, thanks, Mormons. Another mall parking garage with an angel on top. You've answered the design question no one was asking: "What if we up-lit a Soviet-era apartment complex?" "Our religion isn't strange at all. Now, please, step inside our windowless box of creepy."

INSECT ASIDE

New Rule: Ants have to stop bragging about being able to lift five times their body weight. Fuck you, ant. And by the way, you can wear all the black you want; you still have a fat ass.

ISLAM FOR DUMMIES

New Rule: If your people are so desperate that mannequins make them horny, there's something wrong with your religion. This week, police in Iran confiscated sixty-five mannequins for being too sexy. Guys, I'm sorry, but it's the mannequins that are supposed to have the sticks up their asses. In the free West, we don't have impure thoughts about inert hunks of tit-shaped plastic. We have Britney Spears.

DEATH TO MOOCHY

New Rule: Stop pretending that other governments have nothing to teach us. From those socialists in Sweden, we can learn how to fix a banking crisis. And from our friends in China, we can learn how to punish the jerks who caused it. The ones who took bailout money and bought private jets made out of rubies and veal. Dick Fuld of Lehman Brothers personally made $500 million in subprime mortgages, and he gets to keep it. While you and I pay off his bad bets. Bernie Madoff stole $50 billion, mostly from Jews. For Jews, this was the worst pyramid scheme since the actual pyramids.

Which brings me back to China. A couple of months ago, some greedy businessmen in China were caught spiking the milk they sold to children with melamine, a plastic derivative that boosted the protein levels and thus their profits. You know what the Chinese are doing to the businessmen behind their milk scandal? They're putting them to death. Talk about lactose intolerant.

Now, am I saying we should treat the bankers who poisoned our financial markets with tainted investments the way China treated its poisoners? Please, we're not China. We're just owned by China. So no, I don't think we should put all the bankers to death. Just two. I mean, maybe it's not technically legal, but let's look at the upside. If we killed two random rich, greedy pigs, and I mean killed, like blew them up at halftime of next year's Super Bowl or left them hanging on the big board at the New York Stock Exchange—you know, as a warning, with their balls in their mouth—I think it would really make everyone else sit up and take notice.

This crisis is rooted in greed, and if two deaths shocked a society of three hundred million into acting decently enough to avoid this in the future—well, they'd die as heroes. It's not like collateral damage isn't built into our assessment of things. Cars kill almost fifty thousand people a year, but we accept that as a fair price for being able to get around without riding on top of an animal. So two dead bankers really starts to look like a bargain, and isn't that what they loved—bargains?

—February 20, 2009

J

JAPANESE ZERO

New Rule: Newspapers must get rid of the Sudoku puzzle. Yes, it's big in Japan, but so is Tom Waits. Maybe in Japan they think it's fun to make a bunch of numbers add up, but in America we call that math, and that's a job for India.

JERK ETHIC

New Rule: Powerball jackpot winners must stop saying they're not sure if they're going to quit their jobs. Of course you're going to quit your job. And I have news for you: Your coworkers *want* you to quit your job. Nobody wants to be on the pork-processing line next to the unbearable ass in the Gucci smock.

JERSEY SNORE

New Rule: People on reality shows have to quit saying, "You either love me or you hate me." There's actually a third option: not giving a shit about you.

JHERI-CURLING

New Rule: No black athletes in the Winter Olympics. There's a reason we schedule these things in the cold and snow—so the tropical people won't show up and kick our ass. Look, you've got football, basketball, the presidency. Is it too much to leave us the ice dancing?

BOY BLUNDER

New Rule: Republicans must stop pitting the American people against the government. Last week, we heard a speech from Republican leader Bobby Jindal—and he began it with the story that every immigrant tells about going to an American grocery store for the first time and being overwhelmed with the "endless variety on the shelves." And this was just a 7-Eleven—wait till he sees a Safeway. The thing is, that "endless variety" exists only because Americans pay taxes to a government, which maintains roads, irrigates fields, oversees the electrical grid, and everything else that enables the modern American supermarket to carry forty-seven varieties of frozen breakfast pastry.

Of course, it's easy to tear government down—Ronald Reagan used to say the nine most terrifying words in the English language were "I'm from the government and I'm here to help." But that was before "I'm Sarah Palin, now show me the launch codes."

The stimulus package was attacked as typical "tax and spend"—like repairing bridges is left-wing stuff. "There the liberals go again, always wanting to get across the river." Folks, the people are the government—the first responders who put out fires—that's your government. The ranger who shoos pedophiles out of the park restroom, the postman who delivers your porn.

How stupid is it when people say, "That's all we need: the federal government telling Detroit how to make cars or Wells Fargo how to run a bank. You want them to look like the post office?"

You mean the place that takes a note that's in my hand in L.A. on Monday and gives it to my sister in New Jersey on Wednesday, for 44 cents? Let me be the first to say, I would be thrilled if America's health-care system was anywhere near as functional as the post office.

Truth is, recent years have made me much more wary of government stepping aside and letting unregulated private enterprise run things it plainly is too greedy to trust with. Like Wall Street. Like rebuilding Iraq.

Like the way Republicans always frame the health-care debate by saying, "Health-care decisions should be made by doctors and patients, not government bureaucrats," leaving out the fact that health-care decisions aren't made by doctors, patients, or bureaucrats; they're made by insurance companies. Which are a lot like hospital gowns—chances are your ass isn't covered.

—March 6, 2009

JOHN HANCOCK BLOCK

New Rule: You can't bum-rush the president for autographs after he just lectured you for an hour about how you have to grow up. Have some dignity, for Christ's sake. He's your coworker, not Hannah Montana. If you're this crazy about him now, what are you going to do if he turns the country around, ask him to sign your tit?

JOY RODGERS

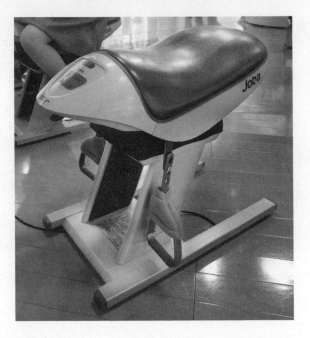

New Rule: Stop pretending this is an exercise machine. The newest "fitness" craze in Japan is the Joba, a horseback-simulation machine. Doesn't anyone in that country just fuck anymore?

JUDGE DELETE-O

New Rule: Stop asking the Supreme Court to rule on stuff they don't understand. First, it was e-mail, now it's violent video games. What are they going to take up next, whether you can follow someone on Twitter who's defriended you on Facebook? Sexting? These justices are so old, Justice Kennedy's idea of cybersex is tapping out "Who's your daddy?" in Morse code.

JUGGER NOT

New Rule: Meteorologists must come up with a new size for hail besides "golf ball," "baseball," and "grapefruit." I wanna hear the weatherman say, "This week in Norman, Oklahoma, they got hail the size of Katy Perry's tits."

DEPLOY, VEY!

New Rule: Forget bringing the troops home from Iraq. We need to get the troops home from World War II. Can anybody tell me why, in 2009, we still have more than sixty thousand troops in Germany and thirty thousand in Japan? At some point, these people are going to have to learn to rape themselves. Our soldiers have been in Germany so long they now wear shorts with black socks. You know that crazy soldier hiding in the cave on Iwo Jima who doesn't know the war is over? That's *us*.

Bush and Cheney used to love to keep Americans all sphinctered-up on the notion that terrorists might follow us home. But actually, we're the people who go to your home and then never leave. Here's the facts: The Republic of America has more than five hundred thousand military personnel deployed on more than seven hundred bases, with troops in one hundred fifty countries—we're like McDonald's with tanks—including thirty-seven European countries—because you never know when Portugal might invade Euro Disney. And this doesn't even count our secret torture prisons, which are all over the place, but you never really see them until someone brings you there—kinda like IHOP.

Of course, Americans would never stand for this in reverse—we can barely stand letting Mexicans in to do the landscaping. Can you imagine if there were twenty thousand armed Guatemalans on a base in San Bernardino right now? Lou Dobbs would become a suicide bomber.

And why? How did this country get stuck with an empire? I'm not saying we're Rome. Rome had good infrastructure. But we are an empire, and the reason is because once America lands in a country, there is no exit strategy. We're like cellulite, herpes, and Irish relatives: We are not going anywhere. We love you long time!

—March 27, 2009

K

KEGGER, PLEASE

New Rule: No more studies warning us about how college students are binge drinking. What other kind of drinking do you think twenty-year-olds are doing, wine tasting? Of course they're binge drinking. Hell, with this job market waiting for them, just be happy they're not breaking into your house and stealing your prescription drugs.

KEYSTROKE

New Rule: If you are tweeting more than ten times a day, you need to take up a more productive hobby. Like masturbating. Look at it this way, it's slightly better exercise, and you'll be giving pleasure to the exact same number of people.

KFU

New Rule: Kentucky Fried Chicken can call their roadkill whatever they want. I'm still not eating out of a bucket. This week, for the fourth time, KFC is introducing "grilled" chicken. I'm sorry, but you're missing the whole reason my mouth's not watering: The problem isn't the word "fried." It's the word "Kentucky."

KID RATION

New Rule: Crap peddlers must stick to selling crap. Burger King has made their Kids Meals healthier—and not just by removing the toy from China. The new, healthier Kids Meal includes broiled chicken, organic applesauce, and low-fat milk. You also get a moist towelette for quick cleanup after your kid freaks out and dumps the whole thing in your car.

KIDDIE LITTER

New Rule: If you get to bring your baby into the public swimming pool, I get to follow you home and piss in his bathwater.

STAR DREK

New Rule: Human beings are such slobs, from now on pigs must declare us the other white meat. Do you know that right now there's so much discarded trash in outer space that three times last month the international space station was almost hit by some useless hunk of floating metal, not unlike the international space station itself? Really, you've got to give the human race credit. Only humans could visit an infinite void and leave it cluttered. Not only have we screwed up our own planet, somehow we've also managed to use up all the space in . . . space.

History shows over and over again that if the citizens of earth put their minds to it, they can destroy anything. It doesn't matter how remote or pristine, together, yes, we can *fuck it up*. The age of space exploration is only fifty years old, and we have already managed to turn the final frontier into the New Jersey Meadowlands. You know what's up there? Old satellites, spent rocket boosters, Neil Armstrong's golf club, that canister with Gene Roddenberry's ashes, empty Tang jars, discarded astronaut diapers—more than one hundred thousand items, my favorite being a NASA space glove, which in 1965 was lost by astronaut Ed White. I can't tell you why he had his glove off, except to say that in space, it can get very lonely.

The reason this is so worrisome is something called the Kessler syndrome, wherein the more debris there is flying around, the more collisions occur, which exponentially expands the amount of debris, making it impossible to keep satellites up there . . . pretty soon we lose the cell phone networks, and then we face a world where teenagers are forced to send one another pictures of their genitals by mail.

Of course, the other seemingly limitless expanse we've endangered lately is the ocean. Which we're killing. Why? Because the Bible says God gave us dominion over the earth—which is taken to mean that God was saying, "This is your rental car—taketh it, and beateth the shit out of it. For who careth, it is a rental."

Did you know that there is now floating in the Pacific Ocean a 3.5-million-ton island of shit made up of all the indestructible crap we toss away, the stuff that will never break down, like Styrofoam and old Clorox bottles. And it's twice the size of Texas—that's right, the Pacific Ocean now contains more white trash than Texas.

—April 3, 2009

KILL THE EMPIRE

New Rule: Americans have to stop saying we don't have an exit strategy in Libya. Please. Look at Japan, Germany, Korea, Iraq, Afghanistan. We're still in all those places. But we're not in Vietnam or Somalia. So clearly we do have an exit strategy. It's called "losing."

KILLY OCEAN

New Rule: Stop asking why the killer whale killed the lady. Why do you think? He was denied tenure? Killer whales kill. Hence the name "killer whale." And, guys, before you get any ideas, stay away from the blowfish.

KIM JONG ILL

New Rule: Let's end the debate over whether North Korea has weapons that constitute a "direct threat." If you don't think Korea has access to dangerous toxic chemicals, you've obviously never been to a strip-mall nail salon.

KITTY PORN

New Rule: If you want to send me a link, you must take the extra five seconds to tell me what it is. How do I know if I'm going to see some adorable kittens at play or a piece of truly disgusting fetish porn that will be burned into my brain for the rest of my life? I need that info, because, really, at this point, I've seen plenty of kittens.

KOBE BEEF

New Rule: The Japanese must invent one thing that's not at least vaguely pornographic.

KVETCH OF THE DAY

New Rule: Israel has to stop being mad at Obama because he won't plan a visit. We're your ally. Not your grandchildren. Calm down and give it a rest, or you'll get Biden again.

SENIOR MOMENT

New Rule: Stop making college students sit through commencement speeches. You've just gone years in debt for a worthless diploma, now here's your reward: twenty minutes of motivational bullshit from Coach Bobby Knight. I firmly believe if college students wanted to hear more drivel they're never going to use again, they could go to class. So I would tell this graduating class exactly what they have to look forward to: working at Starbucks. I'm joking, of course. Starbucks isn't hiring. Here's the speech I would give.

Graduates, faculty, alumni, and guests, I am truly honored to speak at your university, mostly because it's a great place to score cheap weed. I've been asked by your dean to keep it brief, and by your feminist studies club to keep it humorless. So class of 2009, as you go out in the world, here is my message for you: Give up. You're about to enter the worst job market since Adam and Eve hired the very first employee, a Mexican to tend their garden. On top of that, you went through the American educational system. You wrote "Hi, Mom!" on your cap, and you spelled "Hi" wrong.

And if all that wasn't enough, you are the first generation to inherit an environment that's probably already toast, but, hey, maybe you can make a few bucks smearing sunscreen on old people. Just remember, there's more to life than work. Maybe now's the time to appreciate the little things. A flower. A sunset. A shopping cart full of cans.

So I say to you as you embark on your new adult life, take a moment to look back and honor your parents. Because they're the ones who paid for your education; they're the ones who stood by you the whole time. And they're the ones you'll be moving back in with in the fall.

So look at them—look at your parents right now. Or, more likely, your dad and his new wife, who's your age, and your mom and her new boyfriend, whom she met on Myspace. And after the ceremony, I want you to take them aside and say something very important to them: "This is your fault!" Who do you think it was who tanked the economy and spent all the money and melted the planet and let the schools rot? Yes, it was us, but at least I hope we taught you that in life, there really is no such thing as failure, because if there were, we wouldn't be seeing Dick Cheney on TV every day. In closing, remember above all that no matter where life takes you, you will always have something deep inside you of great value: plasma.

—May 15, 2009

LEFT, RIGHT, AND VENTER

New Rule: He's your president, not your boyfriend. Last week I criticized President Obama for not fighting corporate influence enough, and it made some liberals very angry. My phone rang off the hook, my e-mail filled up, and Nancy Pelosi got so mad, her face moved. Look, I like Obama, too, I'm just saying, let's not make it a religion. And as far as you folks on the right who think we're somehow now in league . . . We're not in league. I was criticizing Obama for not being hard *enough* on the corporate douche bags you live to defend. I don't want to be on your team; pick another kid. So I stand by my words, but there is another side to the story, and that is that every time Obama tries to take on a progressive cause, there's a major political party standing in his way. The Democrats.

People talk a lot about a third political party in America. We don't need a third party, we need a *first* party.

This is because we don't have a left and a right party in this country anymore. We have a center-right party, and a crazy party. Over the last thirty-odd years, Democrats have moved to the right, and the right has moved into a mental hospital. So what we have is one perfectly good party for hedge-fund managers, credit-card companies, banks, defense contractors, big agriculture, and the pharmaceutical lobby—that's the Democrats. And they sit across the aisle from a small group of religious lunatics, flat earthers, and Civil War reenactors who mostly communicate by AM radio and call themselves the Republicans, and who actually worry that Obama is a socialist. Socialist? He's not even a liberal.

I know he's not, because he's on TV. And while I see Democrats on television, I don't see actual liberals. And if occasionally you do get to hear Ralph Nader or Noam Chomsky or Dennis Kucinich, they're treated like buffoons. Okay, these are not three of the world's most charismatic men, but then nobody's ever going to confuse Newt Gingrich for Zac Efron, and I have to look at his fat face on TV more often than that "free credit report" song.

Shouldn't there be one party that unambiguously supports cutting the military budget? A party that is straight up in favor of gun control, gay marriage, higher taxes on the rich, universal health care, legalizing pot, and steep, direct taxing of polluters?

These aren't radical ideas. A majority of Americans are either already for them, or would be if they were properly argued and defended. And what we need is an actual progressive party to represent the millions of Americans who aren't being served by the Democrats. Because bottom line: Democrats are the new Republicans. It's like when some Chinese company buys the name of a great old American brand and slaps it on some cheap crap. You buy it out of reflex, and it's only later that you think, "Wow, I didn't even know Woolworth's made dildos."

—*June 19, 2009*

LAMEY POLLER

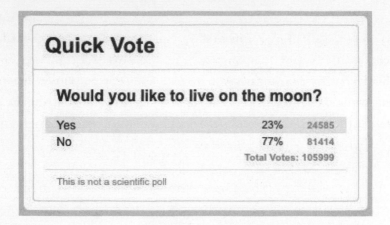

New Rule: If the guy who makes up the poll questions at CNN doesn't want to do it anymore, he should just quit. This is an actual recent poll question: "Would you like to live on the moon?" And the shocking results: No, as it turns out, we would not like to live on the moon. This is the cable news equivalent of being in a dead-end relationship with an idiot. "What are you thinking?" "I dunno, honey. I guess I was just wondering how many Americans would like to live on the moon."

LA TOYA STORY

New Rule: The Jacksons must trot out at least one family member who doesn't make us all ask, "What went on in that house?"

LEAKY CONDIMENT

New Rule: Someone has to make a mustard container that doesn't squirt out yellow water before it gets to the actual mustard. I get all excited for lunch, and then Grey Poupon pees on my sandwich. I suppose I could shake the bottle first, but fuck you, I'm an American consumer. Not only should your mustard be pre-blended to my specifications, it should also whiten my teeth.

LETTER RIP

New Rule: You don't need a paper shredder. I've seen your mail—it's not that interesting. What are you worried about, that the magazine from the auto club might fall into the wrong hands? I hate to break it to you, 007, but the Victoria's Secret catalog isn't actually a secret.

LIGHT MY IRE

New Rule: Bring back lamps where the switch is on the actual lamp and not three feet down the cord. How come we used to be able to make lamps with an on/off switch where you'd naturally look for it . . . You know, on the part I like to call "the lamp" . . . but now it's on the cord? Did we lose the technology? I'm going to fight this. I'm going to bring back the lamp with the switch where it belongs. Or my name's not Andy Rooney.

LILO & SCOTCH

New Rule: Now that I've collected all four mug shots, someone has to tell me how I get my free drink at SkyBar.

LIQUOR ASS

New Rule: We can't have fraternities and also sell whiskey in a can. Yes, there's a new offering from Scottish Spirits—eight shots of whiskey, straight up, in a can. Or, as they call it in Ireland, "A cool one." Look, it won't be long before some rich fraternity asshole is shot-gunning this thing, crushing it against his forehead, and then collapsing and dying. So on second thought, New Rule: The whiskey can is cool with me.

LOSER FRIENDLY

New Rule: Apple's next device must be a computer that you control with your tongue. Thanks for eliminating the keyboard and the mouse, but pointing and pushing at things already seems too complicated and tiring. We're Americans—and until you free our hands from the computer entirely, we can never attain our ultimate goal: Web surfing while eating and masturbating.

LOWENBRAU HUMOR

New Rule: Just because you're drunk and it's October, it doesn't make it Octoberfest. When you drink in November, it's not Novemberfest. It's just Thanksgiving, and you hate your relatives. Besides, we already know what happens when people get drunk and start acting like Germans:

LUST DESSERTS

New Rule: Women have to stop having food orgasms. I've heard many women ask, "Why don't they make a Viagra for women?" They do. It's called an M&M. There's nothing more humiliating than being in bed with a woman, and she calls out another man's name, and it's Willy Wonka.

M

MOURNING IN AMERICA

New Rule: All the good news stories have to stop breaking while I'm on vacation. I go away for a mere three weeks to work with my charity, Hot Tubs Without Borders, and Karl Malden dies. But also Michael Jackson, the most famous white lady to die since Princess Diana. And one question gnawed at me the whole time: Why? Why did America lose its collective shit over Michael Jackson? And then, like Michael's father, Joe, it hit me: Michael Jackson *is* America. We love him so much because he reflects our nation perfectly: fragile, overindulgent, childish, in debt, on drugs, and over the hill.

Now, let me state, I don't wish my country was all of these bad things, I just don't want to be like one of those people Michael Jackson had around him, the ones who just tell you you're great and that your destructive behavior is totally normal, and they give you whatever you want—you know, doctors. So let's go down the list and see if I'm crazy or if indeed America is unfortunately all the things that Michael Jackson was.

- *Is America fragile?* What do you think would happen if there was another terrorist attack here? We'd repeal the rest of the Bill of Rights, forget about health care, elect Toby Keith president—and fire me. Are we fragile? The stock ticker in Times Square yesterday said, "What the fuck are you looking at?"
- *Overindulgent*: I defy anyone to watch ten minutes of *My Super Sweet 16* on MTV and not want to strap on a vest and blow up that little snot's birthday party. Did you know that a third of children in America are overweight? Michael Jackson didn't have a heart attack, his playdate rolled over on him.
- *Childish*: Well, we think *Harry Potter* is literature and Batman movies are profound meditations on the human condition. Our morning coffee has become a milk shake with whipped cream,

and sixty-four percent of the population believes Noah's Ark actually happened. And what could be more childish than what our news media chooses to cover? My God, since this Michael Jackson thing happened, I have no idea what's going on with Jon and Kate.

- *In debt*: Please. The deficit—that's just what we run up for the year—is over one trillion dollars. To give you an idea how much that is, take what your home is now worth and add . . . one trillion dollars.
- *On drugs*: If you don't think America's got a drug problem, you must be high. Children are on Prozac, athletes are on steroids. The pharmaceutical industry sold $291 billion worth of pills last year—and that's not counting the potheads and the drinkers— yes, America is on drugs! And by the way, people also do just as much coke as they ever did, they just don't share it anymore.
- *And finally*: Is America over the hill? I don't know. I hope not— but Monday is the fortieth anniversary of Neil Armstrong's first setting foot on the moon, and I can't think of any ambitious goal we've reached since then. It's sad when your peak was a moonwalk that occurred decades ago.

So America faces a choice: We can go the Michael route and keep living on debt and the world's affection for our early work, or we can get our shit together like Britney Spears, put on our circus costume, and go out there and show the world we can still bring it.

—July 17, 2009

MALLOW DRAMA

New Rule: Someone must x-ray my stomach to see if the Peeps I ate on Easter are still in there, intact and completely undigested. And I'm not talking about this past Easter. I'm talking about the last time I celebrated Easter, in 1962.

M.D. PROMISES

New Rule: Sometimes it's better to just stay sick. Doctors say they can cure some intestinal diseases by inserting a healthy person's feces up your butt. Or, as John Travolta calls it, dating. The only thing that's worse than this procedure is asking someone to donate. How do you bring this up on the golf course? *Hey, remember that time I loaned you a hundred bucks?*

MEANY BOPPER

New Rule: Fashion models must lose the disinterested sneer. That look doesn't say "pouty mystique"; it says "I have rectal itch." I know it sucks to be sixteen and stuck on a runway in Milan in a Versace original, but consider the outfit you could be wearing:

MEH AT WORK

New Rule: When I see one of those road signs for the Recovery Act, I should also see people in hard hats building shit. Dig a hole and fill it up with dead bodies, I don't care. I'm just getting tired of passing these randomly placed signs while the gaping potholes shake the fillings out of my skull. It's this kind of crap that makes me want to join the Tea Party. Then I remember I have a high school diploma, a functioning penis, and a black friend.

MEMORY LAME

New Rule: No. The only person who ever missed you is the Iraqi guy who threw the shoe.

MEXICAN'T

New Rule: If Latino immigrants want to be taken seriously, they have to stop wearing the giant hats. The civil rights marchers in the '50s didn't dress like Buckwheat and carry watermelons. You're a proud immigrant demanding his rights, not the Frito Bandito.

MEXICO SHITTY

New Rule: Mexico is closed until further notice. I don't wanna say that country is too dangerous, but the new warning to travelers is: "Don't drink the water—use it to clean your stab wounds." Even Mexicans are frightened of Mexico. At last weekend's sex show in Tijuana, the girl asked the donkey to just hold her.

MILEY HIGH

New Rule: Miley Cyrus must stop wasting our time and just skip to the part where she gets pregnant, loses the baby weight, finds Jesus, gains it all back, switches to Christian rock, goes into rehab, marries her driver, plays Rizzo in *Grease*, and takes her shirt off in the reboot of *Leprechaun, Leprechaun 2031: The Terror of the Trailer Park.*

MOCK BLOCKER

New Rule: You can't use sarcasm about people who think you're an idiot if you're an idiot. Britney Spears went on a sarcastic screed about people who think she needs help. Then her dress fell off, she carved a swastika into her forehead, and ran over her tits with a car. Which raises a question that's been bothering me for some time: Can you un-masturbate to someone?

New Rule: TV networks must combine all of their cooking contests, dieting shows, and talent competitions into one huge reality show that people would truly want to see.

MOURNING WOOD

New Rule: Someone needs to explain to the eighteen-year-old Russian girl who's dating Ron Wood that he's not Mick Jagger. It's an honest mistake, Ekaterina Ivanova, and you're not the first part-time model from Moscow to make it. If you girls would just buy the CDs instead of downloading them illegally, you'd know what the Rolling Stones looked like.

MOZZARELIC

New Rule: Pizza joints must stop hanging pictures of Z-level celebrities on their walls. It doesn't impress me that twelve years ago *21 Jump Street*'s Richard Grieco stopped in for a slice. Especially since he's working here now.

MY FAVORITE MARTIN

New Rule: Someone has to decide whether it's okay to say "Happy Martin Luther King Day." Is it a somber remembrance or an excuse to take the day off and get hammered? Like Memorial Day. And let me remind those who fought it that MLK Day is a real holiday, and not just something black people made up. That's Kwanzaa.

FALSE PROFIT

New Rule: Not everything in America has to make a profit. If conservatives get to call universal health care "socialized medicine," I get to call private, for-profit health care "soulless vampire bastards making money off human pain." Now, I know what you're thinking: "But, Bill, the profit motive is what sustains capitalism." Yes, and our sex drive is what sustains the human species, but we don't try to fuck *everything*.

It wasn't that long ago that when a kid in America broke his leg, his parents took him to the local Catholic hospital, the nun stuck a thermometer in his ass, the doctor slapped some plaster on his ankle, and you were done. The bill was $1.50; plus, you got to keep the thermometer.

But like everything else that's good and noble in life, some bean counter decided that hospitals could be big business, so now they're not hospitals anymore; they're Jiffy Lubes with bedpans. The more people who get sick, and stay sick, the higher their profit margins, which is why they're always pushing the Jell-O.

Did you know that the United States is ranked fiftieth in the world in life expectancy? And the forty-nine loser countries where they live longer than us? Oh, it's hardly worth it, they may live longer, but they live shackled to the tyranny of nonprofit health care. Here in America, you're not coughing up blood, little Bobby, you're coughing up freedom.

The problem with President Obama's health-care plan isn't socialism. It's capitalism. When did the profit motive become the only reason to do anything? When did that become the new patriotism? Ask not what you could do for your country, ask what's in it for Blue Cross Blue Shield.

And it's not just medicine—prisons also used to be a nonprofit business, and for good reason—who the hell wants to own a prison? By definition, you're going to have trouble with the tenants. It's not a coincidence that we outsourced running prisons to private corporations and then the number of prisoners in America skyrocketed.

There used to be some things we just didn't do for money. Did you know, for example, there was a time when being called a "war profiteer" was a bad thing? FDR said he didn't want World War II to create one millionaire, but I'm guessing Iraq has made more than a few executives at Halliburton into millionaires. Halliburton sold soldiers soda for $7.50 a can. They were honoring 9/11 by charging like 7-Eleven. Which is wrong. We're Americans; we don't fight wars for money. We fight them for oil.

And my final example of the profit motive screwing something up that used to be good when it was nonprofit: TV news. I heard all the news anchors this week talk about how much better the news coverage was back in Cronkite's day. And I thought, "Gee, if only you were in a position to do something about it."

—July 24, 2009

N

NAG THE DOG

New Rule: If you're one of the one-in-three married women who say your pet is a better listener than your husband, you talk too much. And I have some bad news for you: Your dog's not listening, either; he's waiting for food to fall out of your mouth.

NAP/TUCK

New Rule: We don't need a picture book about plastic surgery. *My Beautiful Mommy* is the new book written to prepare kids for that magical day when Mommy comes home from the doctor and they don't recognize her. Which is when Mommy should explain to the kids that after giving birth to them and nursing them, her mommy parts needed a little sprucing up. And since it's their fault, it's coming out of their college fund.

NEIGH MEANS NO

New Rule: If you get busted for having sex with a horse and then a year and a half later you decide, "You know what? I'd like to have sex with a horse again," pick a different horse. Play the field. Literally. All I'm saying is there are plenty of fish in the sea. Not to give you any ideas.

NIX CANON

New Rule: Pick a century! You can't submit to complete subjugation *and* be into digital photography. "Remind me to upload these images as jpegs before tomorrow's stoning." Or at least stick to a regular film camera. It's less progressive, and developing the pictures is no problem when you're wearing a darkroom.

NOM DE GRRR

New Rule: The Pentagon has to stop naming military operations. Libya is Operation Odyssey Dawn. What does that mean? Why name these things in the first place? It's teenage bravado, like giving a nickname to your penis. Although, ironically, the nickname for *my* penis is Operation Odyssey Dawn.

NOTES ON A SANDAL

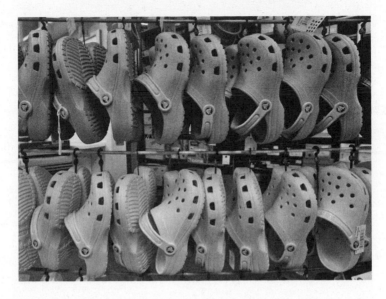

New Rule: Stop wearing plastic shoes. A year ago, only preschoolers and mental patients wore these, but now grown-ups all over America have gone Croc crazy—the latest step in our unending quest to dress as casually as humanly possible. "I used to wear flip-flops, but they're a little dressy. I want clothing I can hose down." Admit it, we're a nation of slobs who won't be happy until we can go to the mall in a diaper.

NOTHING BUT NYET

New Rule: While you're telling me how your March Madness bracket is doing, you also must fill me in on your vacation and show me pictures of your kids. That way, I can not give a shit all at once.

NOYZ N THE HOOD

New Rule: Garbage trucks get to back up without beeping. I'm trying to sleep. You're a giant, churning, groaning behemoth, and when you go backward, it's at one mile per hour while making the sound of Fran Drescher with her hand caught in the blender. If there's anyone out there who can manage to get run over under those conditions, well, you won't just be letting me sleep, you'll be improving the species.

NURSE TACKY

New Rule: And I shouldn't have to say this, but no, God does not want you to breast-feed your coworkers. A new fatwa in Saudi Arabia declares that women should breast-feed their male colleagues and acquaintances, in order to establish "maternal relations" and thus preclude the possibility of sexual contact. Because, really, nothing says "Let's just be friends" like putting your titty in someone's mouth.

NURSERY CRIME

New Rule: If you get to bring your baby to work, I get to bring a Mexican mariachi band. The only difference? For twenty bucks, I can get the mariachi band to go annoy somebody else.

GRAND KENYAN

New Rule: Never underestimate the ability of a tiny fringe group of losers to ruin everything. We've all been laughing heartily at the wacky antics of the "birthers"—the far-right goofballs who claim Obama wasn't really born in Hawaii, and therefore the job of president goes to the runner-up, Miss California Carrie Prejean. And there's nothing you can do to convince these people—you could hand them, in person, the original birth certificate, with the placenta, and have a video of Obama emerging from the womb with Don Ho singing in the background . . . and they still wouldn't believe it. Hey, birthers, wanna hear my theory? My theory is Obama was born in America, and you were born with the umbilical cord around your neck. I don't know what his mother was doing when she was pregnant, but I'm pretty sure yours was drinking.

Oh, I kid the birthers, and actually, there is one thing that makes me think they could be right: We're Americans; of course we're gonna hire an illegal alien to clean up. I'm joking, of course, and laughing it off has also been the reaction from Democratic leaders so far, proving that Democrats never learn: In America, if you don't immediately kill arrant bullshit, no matter how ridiculous, it can grow and thrive and eventually take over, like crabgrass or Cirque du Soleil. This might be a deluded, time-wasting right-wing obsession, but so was Whitewater, and look where that ended up. Liberals said, "Oh, what're they gonna do, keep expanding the case until they impeach the president over a blowjob?"

I'm telling you, in America, there is no idea so patently absurd that it can't catch on. For example, have you ever met a Mormon? More recently, we had the Swift Boat allegations against John Kerry, making him, a genuine war hero, into a coward in a race against a guy who never left Texas—this was so stupid that Kerry refused to even discuss it. And we all know how well that worked out.

You may ask, how does something as inane as Whitewater or Swift

Boats or the "birther" phenomenon gain traction? I'll tell you how: the same way the story about Elton John almost dying from ingesting too much of Rod Stewart's sperm gained traction in my high school: dummies talking to other dummies. It's just easier now because of the Internet and because our mainstream media does such a lousy job of speaking truth to stupid.

Lou Dobbs said recently, "People are asking a lot of questions about the birth certificate." Yes, the same people who want to know where the sun goes at night, and where to put the stamp on their e-mail. And, Lou, you're their new king. That's why it's so important that we the few, the proud, the "reality-based," attack this stuff before it has a chance to fester and spread. It's not a case of Democrats vs. Republicans. It's sentient beings vs. the Lizard People, and it is to them I offer this deal: I'll show you President Obama's birth certificate when you show me Sarah Palin's high school diploma.

—July 31, 2009

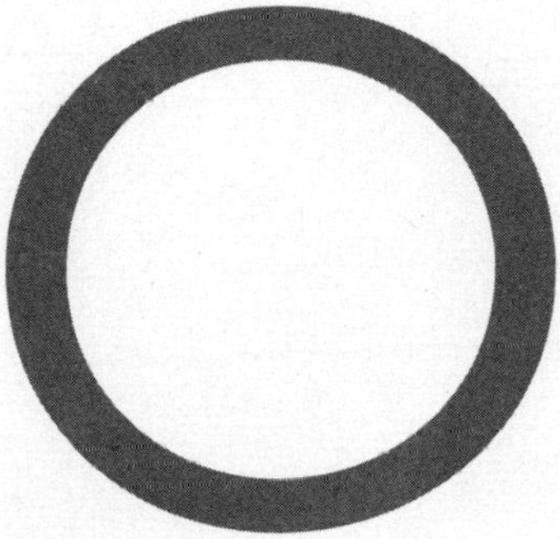

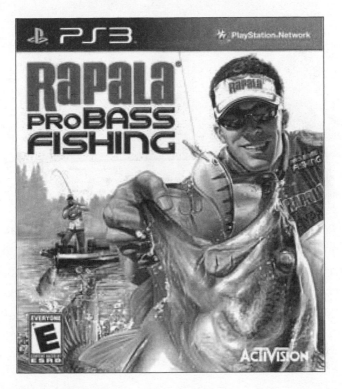

New Rule: Someone has to explain to me the difference between video fishing and just sitting on the couch, drinking beer.

OCTOBER SURMISE

New Rule: Designers of women's Halloween costumes must admit that they're not even trying. They just choose a random profession, like nurse or referee, and put the word "sexy" in front of it, thereby perpetuating the idea of Halloween as a day when normally shy women release their inner sluts and parade around like vixens, and I just completely forgot what I was complaining about.

C TO SHINING C–

New Rule: Just because a country elects a smart president doesn't make it a smart country. A couple of weeks ago, I was asked on CNN if I thought Sarah Palin could get elected president, and I said I hope not, but I wouldn't put anything past this stupid country. Well, the station was flooded with e-mails, and the twits hit the fan. And you could tell that these people were *really* mad, because they wrote entirely in CAPITAL LETTERS!!! Worst of all, Bill O'Reilly refuted my contention that this is a stupid country by calling me a pinhead, which (a) proves my point, and (b) is really funny coming from a doody-face like him.

Now, before I go about demonstrating how, sadly, easy it is to prove the dumbness that's dragging us down, let me just say that ignorance has life-and-death consequences. On the eve of the Iraq War, seventy percent of Americans thought Saddam Hussein was personally involved in 9/11. Six years later, thirty-four percent still do. Or look at the health care debate: At a recent town hall meeting in South Carolina, a man stood up and told his congressman to "keep your government hands off my Medicare," which is kind of like driving cross-country to protest highways.

This country is like a college chick after two Long Island iced teas: We can be talked into anything, like wars, and we can be talked *out* of anything, like health care. We should forget the town halls, and replace them with study halls.

Listen to some of these stats: A majority of Americans cannot name a single branch of government, or explain what the Bill of Rights is. Twenty-four percent could not name the country America fought in the Revolutionary War. More than two-thirds of Americans don't know what's in *Roe v. Wade*. Two-thirds don't know what the Food and Drug Administration does. Some of this stuff you should be able to pick up simply by being alive. You know, like the way the *Slumdog* kid knew about cricket.

Not here. Nearly half of Americans don't know that states have two senators, and more than half can't name their congressman. And among Republican governors, only three got their wife's name right on the first try. People bitch and moan about taxes and spending, but they have no idea what their government spends money on. The average voter thinks foreign aid consumes twenty-four percent of our federal budget. It's actually less than one percent.

A third of Republicans believe Obama is not a citizen, and a third of Democrats believe that George Bush had prior knowledge of the 9/11 attacks, which is an absurd sentence, because it contains the words "Bush" and "knowledge." Sarah Palin says she would never apologize for America. Even though a Gallup poll says eighteen percent of us think the sun revolves around the earth. No, they're not stupid. They're interplanetary mavericks.

And I haven't even brought up religion. But here's one fun fact I'll leave you with: Did you know only about half of Americans are aware that Judaism is an older religion than Christianity? That's right, half of America looks at books called the Old Testament and the New Testament and cannot figure out which one came first.

I rest my case.

—August 7, 2009

OFF-TRACK BEDDING

New Rule: Stop putting all those pillows on the bed. Attention, interior designers, hotel maids, and real housewives of New Jersey: It's a bed, not an obstacle course. I'm sorry, baby, I'd like to make sweet love to you all night long, but by the time I get all that crap off your bed, I'm *exhausted*. A bed needs only two pillows: one to put my head on, and one to cuddle with and pretend it's Robert Pattinson.

ONO YOU DI'N'T

New Rule: Yoko Ono has to stop saying, "It's what John would have wanted." Really? He would have wanted his songs interpreted by Russian gymnasts at the Mirage casino?

He would have wanted a John Lennon action figure?

I think I know what John Lennon would have wanted: a divorce, and Lucy Liu.

ORBITUARY

New Rule: Since our new national position on science is "Screw it; we prefer witchcraft," let's not just retire the Space Shuttle *Atlantis,* let's drive it to one of the five stupidest states and have the locals beat it with sticks. Putting it in a museum is too dangerous. Someone could steal it, fly it into space, and notice we revolve around the sun.

OTTOMAN UMPIRE

New Rule: Stop leaving couches on the sidewalk. Besides being lazy and ugly, it's animal cruelty. You teach your dog not to pee on the couch, and then when you take him to the place he's supposed to pee, there's a couch.

YES, WE CANNED

New Rule: Democrats must get in touch with their inner asshole. I refer
to the case of Van Jones, the man the Obama administration hired to find
jobs for Americans in the new green industries. Seems like a smart thing
to do in a recession, but Van Jones got fired because he got caught on tape
saying Republicans are assholes. And they call it news!

Now, I know I'm supposed to be all reinjected with yes-we-can fever
after the big health-care speech, and it was a great speech—when Black
Elvis gets jiggy with his teleprompter, there is none better. But here's the
thing: Muhammad Ali also had a way with words, but it helped enor-
mously that he could also punch guys in the face.

It bothers me that Obama didn't say a word in defense of Jones and
basically fired him when Glenn Beck told him to. Just like we dropped
"end-of-life counseling" from health-care reform because Sarah Palin
said it meant "death panels" on her Facebook page. Crazy morons make
up things for Obama to do, and he does it.

Same thing with the speech to schools this week, where the president
attempted to merely tell children to work hard and wash their hands, and
Cracker Nation reacted as if he was trying to hire the Black Panthers to
hand out grenades in homeroom. Of course, the White House immediately capitulated. "No students will be forced to view the speech," a White
House spokesperson assured a panicked nation. Isn't that like admitting
that the president might be doing something unseemly? What a bunch of
cowards. If the White House had any balls, they'd say, "He's giving a
speech on the importance of staying in school, and if you jackasses don't
show it to every damn kid, we're cutting off your federal education fund-
ing tomorrow."

The Democrats just never learn: Americans don't really care which side
of an issue you're on as long as you *don't act like pussies.* When Van Jones
called the Republicans assholes, he was paying them a *compliment.* He was

talking about how they can get things done even when they're in the minority, as opposed to the Democrats, who can't seem to get anything done even when they control both houses of Congress, the presidency, and Bruce Springsteen.

I love Obama's civility, his desire to work with his enemies; it's positively Christlike. In college, he was probably the guy at the dorm parties who made sure the stoners shared their pot with the jocks. But we don't need that guy now. We need an asshole.

Mr. President, there are some people who are never going to like you. That's why they voted for the old guy and Carrie's mom. You're not going to win them over. Stand up for the seventy percent of Americans who aren't crazy.

And speaking of that seventy percent, when are we going to actually show up in all this? Tomorrow Glenn Beck's army of zombie retirees is descending on Washington. It's the Million Moron March, although they won't get a million, of course, because many will be confused and drive to Washington state—but they will make news. Because people who take to the streets always do. They're at the town hall screaming at the congressman; we're on the couch screaming at the TV. Especially in this age of Twitters and blogs and Snuggies, it's a statement to just leave the house. But leave the house we must, because this is our last best shot for a long time to get the sort of serious health-care reform that would make the United States the envy of several African nations.

—*September 11, 2009*

P

PAN THEISM

New Rule: There's only one thing to say about the Christian Film and Television Commission giving me the Bigoted Bile Award and naming *Religulous* the number-one Most Unbearable Movie of 2008: Thank you! You hate me, you really hate me!

PANTS, PANTS REVOLUTION

New Rule: Just because I'm in my underwear doesn't mean I'm "parading around." Why is it women always accuse men in their boxers of "parading around in their underwear"? There is no parade. I just happen to be not wearing pants. And if that bothers you so much, maybe you should get off and wait for the next elevator.

PAP SNEER

New Rule: After all the hype for *Toy Story 3*, it must give me an actual Buzz and an actual Woody.

PAPAL TIGER

New Rule: Let the Pope be Pope. An animal-rights group in Italy has asked Pope Benedict to give up his fur-trimmed cape and hat. To which the Pope replied, "Don't be hatin' on my cape, bitch." Sorry, but Popes are the original divas, they invented bling, they've been wearing outlandish outfits for a thousand years—almost as long as Elton John. The clothes, the jewels, the fancy palace . . . Those aren't just symbols of the Papacy, they *are* the Papacy. The day the Pope shows up on the balcony in a pair of jeans and a polo shirt is the day a billion Catholics go, "What the hell were we thinking?"

PARISH IS BURNING

New Rule: If churches don't have to pay taxes, they also can't call the fire department when they catch fire. Sorry, Reverend, that's one of those "services" that goes along with "paying in." I'll use the fire department I pay for. You can pray for rain.

PARISH THE THOUGHT

New Rule: Stop giving churches names like Ecclesia. Ecclesia doesn't sound like a church, it sounds like a tranquilizer for mental cases. On second thought, *all* churches should be named Ecclesia.

PARTICLE BORED

New Rule: Instead of using their $10 billion atom-smashing Large Hadron Collider to re-create the Big Bang by melting atom parts in temperatures a million times hotter than the sun, scientists should *not* do that. I'm just sayin' it sounds dangerous. I'm as interested as the next guy in determining the origin of matter, but first couldn't we solve some simpler mystery, like why smoke-detector batteries always die at four a.m.?

PATIENCE ZERO

New Rule: You can't force the ATM to do something it doesn't want to do. Excuse me, lady in front of me at the Citibank ATM, but you've been standing there punching buttons for ten minutes—what are you trying to do, write a novel on it? You hear those beeping noises? That's the ATM saying, "Stop it, you're hurting me." A chicken would have gotten forty bucks out of that thing by now just by pecking the buttons randomly.

PATIENT ZEROES

New Rule: You don't need to tell me when any of the following people check into a hospital—I'll just go ahead and assume maybe they're already there: David Hasselhoff, Kiefer Sutherland, Nick Nolte, Whitney Houston, Margot Kidder, the Kennedys, Tom Sizemore, Charlie Sheen, whoever's dating Charlie Sheen, and that guy from the *Jackass* movies who went swimming with sharks with shark bait on his dick.

PDA-HOLES

New Rule: Couples who make out in public must bring a bucket along for me to throw up in. I didn't come all the way to Applebee's to be sickened by your dry humping. I came all the way to Applebee's to be sickened by the food.

PEANUTS ENVY

New Rule: I don't need a bigger, "Mega" M&M. If I'm extra-hungry for M&M's, I'll go nuts and eat two.

PEEL TIME

New Rule: Take the stupid "Coexist" bumper sticker off your car. Oh, if only there were a place where Muslims, Christians, and Jews could live together in peace. Actually, there is; it's called Los Angeles, and you're *driving through it.* Try putting that sticker on your rental car in Jordan and see how far you get before your Prius blows up.

PETITION IMPOSSIBLE

New Rule: Activists have to stop preying on my liberal sympathies outside of Whole Foods. I know my signature is vital to the antiwar movement, clean-needle programs, music in schools, a free Tibet, and the fight against autism in gay polar bears, but I just need some hummus and a can of pinto beans—for $37.

PHYSICAL EDUCATION

New Rule: If you're going to have sex with your students, you have to let them up for air. A teacher in Delaware allegedly had sex with her thirteen-year-old student twenty-eight times in one week. Oh, to be young again! I'm getting dehydrated just thinking about it. Jesus Christ, lady. What do you teach, Spanish fly? And, son, if you're out there, Larry Flynt asked me to pass along this message: When you turn eighteen, you've got yourself a job!

PILL MAHER

New Rule: Stop pretending that drugs have an expiration date. So what if the Tylenol expired last year? It's acetaminophen, not egg salad. Besides, the other day I found some mushrooms in a jacket I haven't worn since 1986, and they worked just fine.

PINHEADS

New Rule: If bowling passes for high school athletics, then maybe it is time for a draft. That's right, bowling, an activity that requires rolling a ball without spilling your beer, is America's fastest-growing high school sport. "Congratulations, Tad, you just lettered in fucking off." On the upside, there's nothing like polyester pants and a Ban-Lon shirt to help a guy honor his abstinence pledge.

PLAY D'OH!

New Rule: Don't let the guy who wrote *Glengarry Glen Ross* remake *The Diary of Anne Frank*. David Mamet is writing Anne Frank. He's a great playwright, but I don't need to hear Anne tell her mother, "Fuck *you* I'm staying in this attic, you fucking fuck." Although Pacino could play the hell out of the part.

PORKY DIG

New Rule: Canadian bacon isn't bacon. It's ham. In addition:

Stop letting fifth-grade boys name hot sauces. Is it possible that I might be able to enjoy a touch of habañero without having to read about ass rape, the devil, or death? I'm flavoring my soup, not camping out for tickets to Ozzfest.

POSTPARTUM OBSESSION

New Rule: When I ask how old your toddler is, I don't need to know in months. "Twenty-seven months." "He's two" will do just fine. He's not a cheese. And I didn't care in the first place.

PRO-BUSH

New Rule: You're not posing nude unless I can see your genitals. A peek at Scarlett Johansson's rump isn't good enough, especially when I've had Jake Gyllenhaal's ass in my face twice this year. Which is weird, because I haven't seen *Jarhead* or *Brokeback Mountain*.

New Rule: If America can't get off its back and get something done, it must lose the bald eagle as our symbol and replace it with the YouTube video of the puppy that can't get up. As long as we're pathetic, we might as well act like it's cute.

And I'm sorry, we are pathetic. Inert and lethargic. Unable to end bad things—like wars, farm subsidies, our oil addiction, sixty thousand troops still in Germany, the drug war, useless weapons programs. And unable to initiate anything good—and even when we do address a problem, the plan is always half-assed, and it can never start until years later. Like the climate-change bill in Congress now: It mandates a whopping seventeen percent cut in the greenhouse gas emissions that are killing us . . . *by 2020.* Who's in charge of this program, FEMA? No, really, fellas, don't rush, only the whole western half of the United States has been on fire for a month.

We might pass new mileage standards, but even if we do, they wouldn't start until 2016. In that year, our cars of the future will glide along while achieving a breathtaking thirty-five miles per gallon. My goodness, is that even humanly possible? You socialist dreamer.

"What do we want!? A small improvement! When do we want it!? 2016!"

When it's something for us personally, like a laxative, it has to start working *now.* My TV remote has a button on it now called On Demand. *You get your ass on my TV screen right now, SpongeBob, and make me laugh now!*

But with big, important things, we're that puppy. The president has said about health care, "If we were starting from scratch, then a single-payer system would probably make sense." *So let's start from scratch.*

Instead, we have a crappy lobbyist-written blowjob-to-corporate-America bill, and it doesn't even kick in until 2013, during which time close to two hundred thousand people will die because they're not covered, and three million will go bankrupt from hospital bills. I have a pretty good idea of the Republican plan for the next three years: Don't let Obama do anything. What kills me is: Apparently that's the Democrats' plan, too.

We weren't always like this. In 1965, President Johnson signed Medicare into law, and eleven months later, seniors were receiving benefits. In World War II, FDR converted car companies to making tanks and planes virtually overnight. In one eight-year period, America went from JFK's ridiculous dream of landing a man on the moon to *landing a man on the moon*.

This generation has had eight years just to build something at Ground Zero. An office building, a museum, a Pinkberry, I don't care anymore. America: Home of the Freedom Pit. Which, ironically, is spitting distance from Wall Street, where they knock down buildings a different way—through foreclosure.

That's the ultimate sign of our lethargy: millions thrown out of their homes, tossed out of work, lost their life savings—and they just take it. Thirty percent interest on credit cards? Are you kidding me? It's a good thing for the banks the Supreme Court legalized sodomy.

I still like the president; I can't help liking the president—but what happened to "change," and when did "the fierce urgency of now" become "Your call is important to us, please continue to hold"?

—*September 25, 2009*

PROGNOSTIC-HATER

New Rule: Americans must choose: Either they believe in science or they believe in Punxsutawney Phil. You don't believe in evolution or global warming? In that case, you have to base every decision in your life on a rodent coming out of a hole and seeing its shadow. "Should I get that lump in my testicle looked at? Punxsutawney Phil says no!"

PROJECT SAFEWAY

New Rule: The outside world is not your house. Is it me, or will people wear just about anything to the supermarket? You hear that announcement over the PA: "Cleanup in aisle seven"? They're talking to you! It's heartwarming that you held on to those comfy gym shorts from high school, but I can see your balls. Which reminds me, I'm out of kiwis.

PROPPYCOCK

New Rule: Next year, someone has to put an initiative on the ballot that bans all ballot initiatives. Can you follow these things? "Vote yes to say no to the people who support the opponents of Prop 13 by voting no on Prop 11, which says yes to energy independence and not no to our teachers and firefighters."

PUBIC'S TUBE

New Rule: This better not be a device that allows women to pee standing up. Okay, it is, and it's called the Go Girl. The manufacturers say it's much more sanitary than sitting on a public toilet seat . . . unless you consider the fact that you're walking around with a piss-soaked funnel.

PUMPING IRONER

New Rule: California Republicans shouldn't be mad at Arnold for betraying family values by screwing the maid. They should be mad because he's from Austria, and he was making an anchor baby. I'm not sure what an Austrian/Mexican fifth-grader would sound like, but I think I talked to one when I called AT&T to change my cell-phone plan.

PUMPY LOVE

New Rule: If your blood flow is such that you have to choose between maintaining an erection or your heartbeat, it's time to take off the Snuggie. A new study finds men who sit around and don't exercise are much more likely to have a heart attack during sex. And the heart attack, it turns out, doesn't come from the exertion but from the surprise that anyone is willing to have sex with you.

PUPPY LOVE

New Rule: "Screwing the pooch" is just an expression. A Washington state woman told police she looked out on her back porch to find her husband going at it with the family pit bull. Ooh, that's gotta be a blow to a woman's ego: "My wife/the dog . . . Here, boy!" When will men get it through their heads? Not everyone you buy dinner for has to put out.

JUST SCREW IT

New Rule: Stop saying "sex addict" like it's a bad thing. In the wake of Tiger Woods's heartfelt apology that he gave to his fans, his friends, his foundation—and, just to be safe, Elizabeth Edwards—the media has been interviewing sex addicts: on CNN, one addict said, "The day Mount Saint Helens blew up, everyone was talking about it. But I didn't even know it happened, because I was having sex all that day." Oh, the humanity! Please get this man some professional help soon, before he has a hot three-way and completely misses a tornado.

Now, I haven't commented on Tiger Woods much, because, well, he's just a golfer, and it took me this long to give a shit. But all this talk about sex addiction now—please—sex addiction is just something Dr. Drew made up because he had no other way to explain Andy Dick. And that's not just me saying that—it's also the American Psychiatric Association, which does not list sex addiction in its manual; it does not regard it as a real psychological syndrome, like delirium or bipolar disorder or any of the other things Glenn Beck suffers from.

But before Tiger moves on, there's one more apology he really should make, and that's to Buddha, for dragging him into this mess and proving once again that whenever something unspeakably tawdry, loathsome, and cheap happens, just wait a few days. Religion will make it worse.

Now, usually, when famous cheaters are looking for public redemption, they go to Jesus, but Tiger went old school and claimed that sleeping with two-thirds of the waitresses in America had made him a failure as a Buddhist. He said Buddhism teaches you the way to inner peace is letting go of desire—and if that doesn't sound like marriage, I don't know what does.

Personally, if I were a golfer, I'd go with Jesus—because he's a Trinity, so when you walk with him, you've got a foursome.

Christianity is for rubes. Buddhism is for actors.

And it really is outdated in some ways—the "Life sucks, and then you die" philosophy was useful when the Buddha came up with it around 500 B.C., because back then life pretty much sucked, and then you died, but now we have medicine, and Pinkberry, and TiVo; we have Vegas and Skype—our life isn't all about suffering anymore.

Tiger said, "Buddhism teaches that a craving for things outside ourselves" makes us unhappy, which confirms something I've long suspected about Eastern religions: They're a crock, too.

Craving for things outside ourselves is what makes life *life*—I don't want to learn to *not* want; that's what people in prison have to do. Buddhism teaches that suffering is inevitable. The only thing that's inevitable is that if you have fake boobs and hair extensions, Tiger Woods will try to fuck you.

And reincarnation? Really? If that were real, wouldn't there be some proof by now? A raccoon spelling out in acorns, "My name is Herb Zoller, and I'm an accountant" . . . something?

—February 26, 2010

Q

QUIET RIOT

New Rule: The sad mime at every protest has to give it a rest. One sign you're a major annoyance: when you haven't said anything and I *still* want to tell you to shut the fuck up.

HOLLYWOOD RETORTER

New Rule: Conservatives have to stop complaining about Hollywood values. It's Oscars time again, which means two things: (1) I've got to get waxed, and (2) talk-radio hosts and conservative columnists will trot out their annual complaints about Hollywood: We're too liberal; we're out of touch with the Heartland; our facial muscles have been deadened with chicken botulism; and we make them feel fat. To these people, I say: Shut up and eat your popcorn. And stop bitching about one of the few American products—movies—that people all over the world still want to buy.

Last year, Hollywood set a new box-office record: $16 billion worldwide. Not bad for a bunch of socialists. You never see Hollywood begging Washington for a handout, like corn farmers, or the auto industry, or the entire state of Alaska.

What makes it even more inappropriate for conservatives to slam Hollywood is that they more than anybody lose their shit over any D-lister who leans right to the point that they actually run them for office. Sonny Bono? Fred Thompson? And let's not forget that the modern conservative messiah is a guy who costarred with a chimp. That's right, Dick Cheney.

I'm not trying to say that when celebrities are conservative they're almost always lame, but if Stephen Baldwin killed himself and Bo Derek with a car bomb, the headline the next day would be "Two Die in Car Bombing."

The truth is that the vast majority of Hollywood talent is liberal, because most stars adhere to an ideology that jibes with their core principles of taking drugs and getting laid. The liberal stars that the right is always demonizing—Sean Penn and Michael Moore, Barbra Streisand and Alec Baldwin and Tim Robbins, and all the other members of my biweekly cocaine orgy—they're just people with opinions. None of them hold elective office, and liberals aren't begging them to run. Because we live in the real world, where actors do acting, and politicians do . . . nothing.

We progressives love our stars, but we know better than to elect them. We make the movies here, so we know a well-kept trade secret: Those people on that screen are only *pretending* to be geniuses, astronauts, and cowboys.

So please don't hate on us. And please don't ruin the Oscars. Because honestly, we're just like you: We work hard all year long, and the Oscars are really just our prom night. The tuxedos are scratchy, the limousines are rented, and we go home with eighteen-year-old girls.

—May 3, 2010

R

RACEBOOK

New Rule: We must scour the earth to see if there is anyone more white than Cameron and Tyler Winklevoss. It's like a trust fund had sex with the J.Crew catalog, and this is what happened.

RACK-U-WEATHER

New Rule: And I never thought I'd say this, but the arms race to supply us with hotter, bustier weather women must stop. Either that or at least give me time to reach a climax before you throw to the bald sports guy. I used to tune in to see if I needed a raincoat. Now I wear a raincoat while I'm tuning in.

RAGE AGAINST THE REGIME

New Rule: Anytime you get two million Arabs in a public square and the headline *isn't* "Hundreds Trampled During Religious Festival," that's progress.

RAPTOR'S DELIGHT

New Rule: If you make a plane like the F-22, and they cost $350 million each, and then you have *three* wars, and you still don't use it, you have to admit that the defense budget is really a jobs program. Did we buy this plane as a favor to someone in the office? Is it a supersonic Girl Scout Cookie? Iraq, Afghanistan, Libya . . . Who are we saving it to fight? The Transformers?

READY-TO-SCARE

New Rule: If there really is such a thing as ghosts, they have to be naked. I'll give you that a ghost is a dead soul, returned to torment the living. That makes perfect sense. But how'd he get to keep his pants? Did they die, too? Were his pants also bad in life, and condemned for their pant sins to never find eternal peace? I simply can't accept that any pants could commit a sin so grave that God could not forgive. Except acid-wash jeans.

RENTAL DAMN

New Rule: Netflix has to stop hassling me with e-mails. "Have you received your DVD?" "Have you mailed your DVD yet?" "How was the picture quality of your DVD?" "How would you rate your DVD?" Enough already; Netflix is like a bad girlfriend—always asking pointless questions, and takes two days to come.

RIGHT SAID PED

New Rule: Stop telling me your toddler is going to be a "heartbreaker" or that she's "flirting" with me. It's just creepy. And it makes me regret having lunch alone at a Chuck E. Cheese.

LEARN NOTICE

New Rule: Let's not fire the teachers when students don't learn—let's fire the parents. Last week President Obama defended the firing of every single teacher in a struggling high school in a poor Rhode Island neighborhood. And the kids were outraged. They said, "Why blame our teachers?" and "Who's President Obama?" I think it was Whitney Houston who said, "I believe the children are our future—teach them well and let them lead the way." And that's the last sound piece of educational advice this country has gotten—from a crackhead in the 1980s.

Now, I know what you're saying: "But Bill! What do you know about raising kids? You don't have any." Yeah. I also don't have any fish, but I know not to fill their tank with Mountain Dew. Or to enter a kid in a beauty pageant. Or to let them be an altar boy. And what you do with your spawn affects me. They're the ones who run me over while they're texting, because they're using an online dictionary to spell "Where U at?"

Yes, America has found its new boogeyman to blame for our crumbling educational system. It's just too easy to blame the teachers, what with their cushy teachers' lounges, their fat-cat salaries, and their absolute authority in deciding who gets a hall pass.

But isn't it convenient that once again it turns out that the problem isn't us, and the fix is something that doesn't require us to change our behavior or spend any money. It's so simple: Fire the bad teachers, hire good ones from some undisclosed location, and, hey, while we're at it, let's cut taxes more. It's the kind of comprehensive educational solution that could come only from a completely ignorant people.

Firing all the teachers may *feel* good—we're Americans; kicking people when they're down is what we do—but it's not really their fault. Now, undeniably, there are some bad teachers out there. They don't know the material, they don't make things interesting, they have sex with the same kid every day instead of spreading the love around . . . But every school has crappy teachers. Harvard has crappy teachers—they must, they gave us George Bush.

But according to all the studies, it doesn't matter what teachers do. Although everyone appreciates foreplay. What matters is what parents do. The number-one predictor of a child's academic success is parental involvement. It doesn't even matter if your kid goes to private or public school. So save the twenty grand a year and treat yourself to a nice vacation away from the little bastards.

It's also been proven that just having books in the house makes a huge difference in a child's development. If your home is adorned with nothing but Hummel dolls, DVDs, and bleeding Jesuses, congratulations, you've just given your children the gift of duh. Sarah Palin said recently she wrote on her hand because her father used to do it. I rest my case.

When there are no books in the house, and there are no parents in the house, you know who raises the kids? Television. So maybe the problem isn't the teachers. Maybe it's the nannies:

—*March 12, 2010*

RIND RAGE

New Rule: If you're too lazy to peel your own fruit, get scurvy and die. Hoping to appeal to teenagers who say they're too busy to peel oranges, Sunkist is introducing a new pre-cut, pre-peeled snack version. Not to be outdone, Baskin-Robbins has created a new coneless ice cream that your mother pre-chews and spits down your throat.

ROBO POP

New Rule: Sci-fi nerds must finally accept that if it really was possible for a heartless robot to go back in time and prevent someone from being born . . .

. . . Arnold totally would have done it.

ROCK SUCKERS

New Rule: Coal companies have to stop calling coal "energy." That's like a lumber company calling wood "fire." Or Budweiser calling beer "urine." Okay, that one kind of makes sense.

ROGER & MEA CULPA

New Rule: Michael Moore has to be given a lifetime achievement award to make up for all the members of the Academy who booed him in 2003 for accusing George Bush of going to war based on a "fiction." To all the people that night who said, "Michael picked the wrong place and the wrong time," I say, "So did George Bush."

ROUGH TRADE

New Rule: Ain't no party like a Wall Street party, 'cause a Wall Street party don't stop. If we're really going to reform Wall Street, can we start by figuring out a better way to do business than having a bunch of sweaty guys screaming and waving pieces of paper with numbers on them? This is supposed to be the most sophisticated financial system in the world, and they look like they're trying to lay bets at a cockfight.

RULES OF ENRAGEMENT

New Rule: Stop telling me not to do things I wasn't thinking of doing. Really—we don't add water to soup anymore? There's no smoking on airplanes? Gosh, you take a quick twenty-five-year nap and they change *everything* on you! I'd better get out there and learn about this brave new world, right after I eat one of these fancy mints that came with my new DVD player.

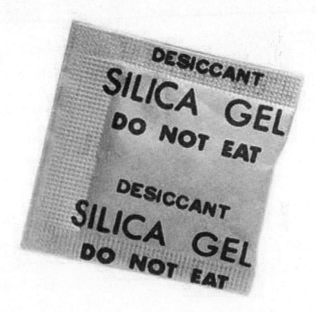

BI-FURIOUS

New Rule: You can't use the statement "There will be no cooperation for the rest of the year" as a threat if there was no cooperation in the first half of the year. Here's a word President Obama should take out of his teleprompter: bipartisanship. People care about that only in theory, not in practice. The best thing that happened this year was when Obama finally realized that and said, "Kiss my black ass, we're going it alone, George W. Bush–style."

Two months ago, conservative Fred Barnes wrote, "The health care bill, ObamaCare, is dead with not the slightest prospect of resurrection." Well, if it's dead, you just got your ass kicked by a zombie named Nancy Pelosi.

And yet even before the Democrats got to take a single victory lap they were being warned not to get drunk with power. I disagree. All you Democrats: Do a shot, and then do another. Get drunk on this feeling of not backing down and doing what you came to Washington to do.

Don't listen to the people who are now saying nothing else big should be attempted for a while, because health care was so rough. Wrong— because I learned something watching the lying bullies of the right lose this one: When they're losing, they squeal like a pig. They kept saying things like the bill was being "shoved down our throats" or the Democrats were "ramming it through." The bill was so big they couldn't take it all at once!

And I realized listening to this rhetoric that it reminded me of something: Tiger Woods's sext messages to his mistress, in which he said, and I quote, "I want to treat you rough, throw you around, spank and slap you and make you sore. I want to hold you down and choke you while I fuck that ass that I own. Then I'm going to tell you to shut the fuck up while I slap your face and pull your hair for making noise." Unquote.

And this, I believe, perfectly represents the attitude Democrats should now have in their dealings with the Republican Party: "Shut the fuck up while I slap your face for making noise—now pass a cap-and-trade law, you stupid bitch, and repeat after me: 'Global warming is real!'"

The Democrats need to push the rest of their agenda while their boot is on the neck of the greedy, poisonous old reptile. Who cares if a cap-and-trade bill isn't popular; neither was health care. Your poll numbers may have descended a bit, but so did your testicles.

So don't stop: We need to regulate the banks; we need to overhaul immigration; we need to end corporate welfare, including at the Pentagon; we need to bring troops home from . . . everywhere; we need to end the drug war; and we need to put terrorists and other human rights violators on trial in civilian courts, starting with Dick Cheney.

Democrats in America were put on earth to do one thing: drag the ignorant hillbilly half of this country into the next century, which, in their case, is the nineteenth—and by passing health care, the Democrats saved their brand. A few months ago, Sarah Palin mockingly asked them, "How's that hopey-changey thing working out for ya?" Great, actually. Thanks for asking. And how's that whole Hooked on Phonics thing working out for you?

—*March 26, 2010*

S

SCARE PIE

New Rule: Domino's Pizza must be renamed The Pizza of Last Resort. Everyone's got their favorite place downtown. If that's closed, you'll go with the frozen one in your freezer. Out of those? You'll make your own pizza out of English muffins and an old bell pepper. It's late, you're drunk, and you've locked yourself out of your apartment? Ah, screw it. Let's order Domino's.

SCHLITZ FOR BRAINS

New Rule: We don't have to play a drinking game—we can just drink. Really. And besides, if I'm hoping your balls land in my beer, I'm already hammered.

SCHLOCK THERAPY

New Rule: Scientists must explain why people will watch crap on Netflix streaming that they would never otherwise watch in a million years. It's like the movie version of picking up some random stranger at a bar at closing time. The whole time you're thinking, "Why am I doing this? I don't even like this movie. I'm a better person than this." And when it's over you take a long shower and tell yourself, "Never again." And then you watch a documentary about lobsters.

SCHNOOKS ON A PLANE

New Rule: If you're stuck on a plane that's not moving for more than five hours, you get to punch a baby.

CARTOON NUTWORK

New Rule: Although America likes to think it's number one, we have to admit we're behind the developing world in at least one thing: Their religious wackos are a lot more wacko than ours. When *South Park* got threatened by Islamists incensed at their depiction of Mohammed, it served—or should serve—as a reminder to all of us that our culture isn't just different than one that makes death threats to cartoonists. It's better. Because when I make a joke about the Pope, he doesn't send one of his Swiss Guards in their striped pantaloons to stick a pike in my ass. When I make a Jewish joke, rabbis may kvetch about it, but they don't pull out a scimitar and threaten an adult circumcision.

It's true: When it comes to scary-ass religions, extremist Muslims are like Godzilla, and we're like *Are You There God? It's Me, Margaret.* Sarah Palin is an evil dingbat who thinks God opens doors, but she never tried to poison-gas a girls' school—as the Taliban does in Afghanistan.

Think about the craziest religious wackos we have here in America. The Mormons. I'm kidding, that's not a religion. No, take the "Christians" who bring their "God hates fags" signs to soldiers' funerals. Now multiply that by infinity and give it an army—that's the Taliban. I've been known to make fun of Christians, but I have the perspective to know they're a lot more evolved than people who target girls for going to school. Why, the worst thing our priests ever do is smother children with kisses.

Even with the latest Catholic horror story, Muslims could teach Christians a clinic in how to be fucked up about sex. That's because Muslims still take their religious leaders seriously, whereas we have the good sense to blow them off. Catholics, for example, don't follow the Pope—in overwhelming numbers they divorce, have premarital sex, and masturbate. And unlike the Koran, no one here seriously considers following the Bible literally—guys don't look over their fence on Sunday morning and see a neighbor mowing the lawn and think, "Working on Sunday? I really should kill him."

Now, Christianity, of course, went through a period like that, where religion had too much influence—it was called the Dark Ages. For centuries, either you joined the Church or you were killed. Nowadays, when a Jehovah's Witness comes to the door, you turn the garden hose on them.

Now, it should in fairness be noted that in speaking of Muslims, we realize that of course the vast majority are law-abiding, loving people who just want to be left alone to subjugate their women in peace. But civilized people don't threaten one another. We sue one another. Threatening is some old-school desert shit, and I'm sorry, you can't bring that to the big city. I'm very glad Obama is reaching out to the Muslim world, and I know Muslims living in America and Europe want their way of life to be assimilated more. But the Western world needs to make it clear some things about our culture are not negotiable and can't change, and one of them is freedom of speech. Separation of church and state is another—not negotiable. Women are allowed to work here, and you can't beat them—not negotiable. This is how we roll—and it's why our system is better, and if you don't get that, and you still want to kill someone over a stupid cartoon, please make it *Garfield*.

—*April 30, 2010*

SEA MINUS

New Rule: In order to save the government some money, let's get rid of the Coast Guard. We already have someone guarding our coast. They're called the Navy. The rest of your job consists of trying to keep Cubans, Haitians, and pot from reaching our shores. And you know how we know you've failed at that? Florida.

SEAT ME

New Rule: Restaurants can't make you wait until the rest of your party has arrived. Any restaurant that makes you wait is calling you a liar. They're saying, *"You* have five friends? Yeah, we'll see." Listen up, Miss Drunk-with-Power restaurant hostess: When I say my friends are on the way, *they're on the way.* So either show me to a table now or this is the last time I celebrate my birthday at Johnny Rockets.

SEVENTH-INNING KVETCH

New Rule: Don't name your kid after a ballpark. Cubs fans Paul and Teri Fields have named their newborn son Wrigley. Wrigley Fields. A child is supposed to be an independent individual, not a means of touting your own personal hobbies. At least that's what I've always taught my kids, Panama Red and Jacuzzi.

SHELL-SHOCKED

New Rule: You don't have to put the shells in with the clams. You don't put the banana peel in the banana cream pie, or the eggshells in an omelet. I'll take your word for it, you got the clams from the ocean. I don't need a plateful of sand and the medical waste to prove it.

SHOCKER MOM

New Rule: Pop star . . . or parent—but not both. We all know that Britney Spears drives with her baby bungee-corded to the roof rack. And this week, Madonna revealed that her daughter is "obsessed" with gays, and asked Madonna if she was gay, because of her infamous smooch with Britney Spears. No, honey, Mommy's not gay—gay is everyone who still goes to Mommy's concerts.

SHORT FUSELAGE

New Rule: Supermodels should not speak to flight attendants. That's what supermodel May Andersen did, and she was deemed "unruly," and got arrested upon landing. Look, supermodels, it doesn't matter what you're saying: "Can I have a pillow?" "I like your shoes." What the flight attendant hears is, "I'm a supermodel and you're not. Let's fight."

SÍ FOOD

New Rule: Instead of feeding your kids the new spaghetti tacos, why not save some time and just dress them in black and send them out to play on the freeway at night?

SÍ MINUS

New Rule: Anti-immigration people have to admit that speaking Spanish is okay when you want something from Latinos. Americans have no trouble taking the time to learn the Spanish words that we like, such as: tequila . . . margarita . . . sangria . . . marijuana . . . and coochi.

SIS BOOM BRA

New Rule: You can't kick a cheerleader off the squad for working at Hooters. But a cheerleader at East Tennessee State was. Hello? That's like call girls looking down on street whores. You're a cheerleader. What part of the Hooters experience is beneath you, the wings? You both wear skimpy outfits and bounce up and down to get the sports fans excited. Just accept what you are: a farm team for strippers.

SIZE MATTERS

New Rule: Food companies must face the facts: One container equals one serving. Look, we're Americans, and that means once we open the bag, there's no stopping us until we're licking stray bits of powdered cheese off the carpet. So stop trying to give us nutritional information based on a fraction of the package. It assumes a talent for two things that we're really not capable of: restraint and math.

SLACKS LIKE ME

New Rule: The L.L.Bean catalog doesn't need to have a black guy in it. I know you're trying to be inclusive, but not once in our nation's history has a black man put on a turtleneck and wrinkle-resistant chinos, slipped on his moose-hide slippers, gone out to the mailbox, and proclaimed, "Yes! The L.L.Bean catalog is here! Now I can get that canoe I've always wanted!"

SLALOM CEREMONY

New Rule: No more ski-slope weddings. Let's remember what a ski-slope wedding, or a skydiving wedding, or an underwater wedding, says: "My love for you is so strong it doesn't warrant a day off from my hobby." On second thought, what better way to celebrate marriage: heading downhill and feeling frigid.

SLAP ON THE BECK

New Rule: Liberals have to stop gloating about Glenn Beck's falling ratings. Just because he's lost a million viewers in six months doesn't mean America is wising up. His average fan was eighty-nine, weighed 250 pounds, and had the blood pressure of the Deepwater Horizon. They didn't tune out, they died.

SLAY STATION

New Rule: Stop saying that violent video games are making our kids violent. It's just not true. Although they are making our kids fat, useless assholes with the social skills of mole rats. But don't worry, little Bobby's not going to take the ax in the garage and slaughter his entire family . . . That would involve getting off the couch.

SO SEUSS ME

New Rule: Conservatives must get back to their core principle of shitting on everything the first lady does. It's been literally *hours* since Michelle Obama read *The Cat in the Hat* to a bunch of schoolchildren. Where's the backlash? What's the matter, did the batshitmobile break down? She was indoctrinating our kids with her Marxist feline feminazi rainy-day socialist funtime propaganda! Come on, wingnuts, this story has everything you hate: powerful black women, public schools, and books.

PEE-PEE WRONG STALKING

New Rule: If a woman rejects your first dozen advances, don't up the ante by sending her a picture of your penis. This week, we found out that Vikings quarterback Brett Favre allegedly tried to get with a young woman by sending her Myspace messages, voicemails, and notes through a friend, and when none of that worked, and it was third and long—though, not as long as most of us would have imagined—he decided to sext her pictures of Little Brett to close the deal. Brett, I get it: Your dictionary doesn't include the word "quit" or "retire" or "married," but you've got to at least understand "punt." You know the worst part about having sex with Brett Favre? He keeps saying he's finished, and then he comes back to drag it out for another year.

To me, this story isn't about sports or sex or how necessary caller ID is—it's about how pathetic and clueless white American males have become. Because the kind of guy who thinks there are women out there who just, cold, want to see your cock is the same kind of guy who thinks Sarah Palin is swell and tax cuts pay for themselves. I will explain that connection further, but first let's just dwell for one more moment on how stupid it is to forget that in 2010 when you text someone a picture of your genitals, you're not just sending it to that person but to every person on the planet who has access to the Internet. Somewhere right now there's a tribesman in Samoa thinking, "Brett Favre is texting a picture of his dick to a woman? *That shit never works.*"

And he's right—no woman in the history of mankind has ever wanted to see a picture of a penis. Go back to the earliest cave paintings. The very first one is of a cock, and after that they're all antelopes and sunrises. But for some reason, men persist. Why? Because men have always been in charge, especially white men. Brett Favre is like a lot of white males: He's owned the world for so long, he's going a little crazy now that he doesn't. Also, like many white men across the country, he lost his job to a Mexican.

If Brett Favre's penis could talk, what would it say? Well, other than, "No photos, please," I think it would say, "I'm not a witch. I'm you." Because for hundreds of years, white penises *were* America. White penises founded America, they made the rules, and they called the shots in the workplace, in the home, and at the ballot box. But now the unthinkable is happening. White penises are becoming the minority: 2010 was the first year in which more minority babies were born in the U.S. than white babies. This is what conservatives are really upset about—that the president is black, and the secretary of state is a woman, and every shortstop is Latino, and every daytime talk-show host is lesbian, and suddenly this country is way off track and needs some serious "restoring." If penises could cry—and I believe they can—then white penises are crying all over America.

   And that's where women like Sarah Palin and Michele Bachmann and Christine O'Donnell come in—the lovely MILFs of the new right. And their little secret is that their popularity comes exclusively from white men. Look at the polling: Minorities hate them, women hate them—only white men like them. I'm no psychiatrist, but I do own a couch, and my theory is that these women represent something those men miss dearly: the traditional idiot housewife. If an election between Obama and Sarah

Palin were held today, and only white men could vote, Sarah Palin would be president.

Did you know that in 1788, when there were four million people in America, only thirty-nine thousand of them—the rich white men—got to vote? That doesn't sound good to you? Well, what if I threw in a picture of my cock? Which brings me back to Brett Favre, and I think it's worth noting that in one of the alleged photos of him, he's pleasuring himself on a bed while wearing Crocs. And if you think about it, is there any better metaphor for the sad state of America today than an over-the-hill white guy lazily masturbating in plastic shoes?

—October 15, 2010

SODA JERKS

New Rule: As far as I'm concerned, Diet Cherry Chocolate Dr Pepper still doesn't have enough shit going on. I need *Caffeine-free* Diet Cherry Chocolate Dr Pepper. No, I need Cool Ranch Extreme Caffeine-free Diet Cherry Chocolate Dr Pepper. *Baked.* And I want a sticker on it, telling kids that drugs are bad.

SQUAWK BLOCKER

New Rule: A dog is the only animal that can get you laid. No offense, parrot guy, but it's just not gonna happen. When women see you, they're not thinking, "I bet that guy is interesting," they're thinking, "That bird better not shit on my dress."

SQUIRTIN' CALL

New Rule: Science has given us the plastic ketchup bottle, the *squeezable* plastic ketchup bottle, and the *upside-down* squeezable plastic ketchup bottle. Now it must create the ketchup bottle that doesn't make a sound like a fart. You're a condiment, not a whoopee cushion. If I want rude noises from vegetables, I'll go to a Tea Party rally.

STATUTORY JAPE

New Rule: Stop putting religious statues on the front lawn. Whoever said there are no virgins left in L.A. has never been to a Mexican neighborhood—there's one in every front yard. At least my lawn jockey is tasteful. Besides, if I want to see the Virgin Mary, I'll . . .

. . . order the grilled cheese.

STATUTORY TAPE

New Rule: From now on, duct tape must be called what it really is—murder tape. A search of the suspected Craigslist Killer's home yielded a firearm, restraints, and duct tape, or, as we call that here in Hollywood, Phil Spector's earthquake kit.

STICKER SCHLOCK

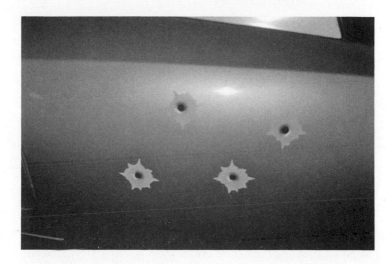

New Rule: Take those fake-bullet-hole decals off your car. Honky, please—this look doesn't say, "I'm a moving target." It says, "I shop at Target."

STUBBLE TROUBLE

New Rule: If your razor has five blades, it's not a razor. It's a weed whacker. With the new Gillette Fusion razor, the first blade lifts the stubble. The second severs the hair follicle. The third slices your skin. The fourth scrapes bone marrow. And the fifth was used by O. J. Simpson to kill his wife, and he wants it back.

STUDENT BOOTY

New Rule: Stop saying that teenage boys who have sex with their hot blond teachers are "permanently damaged." I have a better description of these kids: lucky bastards. I was once beat up after school, and believe me, I would gladly trade that pummeling for a session of oral sex with my French teacher—no matter how much his mustache tickled.

SUNDAY BLUNCH

New Rule: The Chinese community must explain why Chinese restaurants are never open for breakfast. There's a billion of you. You can't all be sleeping in. I'll make you a deal: You tell me why you're not open for breakfast and I'll tell you how to get back on the freeway.

SUNNY AND SHARE

New Rule: Our friends on the East Coast have to forgive us when we laugh at them. Out here, a "rough winter" is when it rains during the Oscars. We don't even need a weather segment on our local news. But we keep it as a jobs program for aging out-of-work actors and Latina girls with big tits.

SWEDE REVENGE

New Rule: Sweden must take a ten-year break from creepy detective novels. Just to replenish your stock of dead women. Your country is smaller than Ohio. You can't *all* be sex murderers, sex-murder victims, politicians covering up sex murders, or alcoholic detectives haunted by childhood memories of sex murders. If you're all dead or drunk, who's gonna make the shitty furniture that breaks when you sit on it?

SWIGGER, PLEASE

New Rule: You don't have to put the cap back on the bottled water after every sip. It's water, not a genie.

New Rule: If you're going to have a rally where hundreds of thousands of people show up, you may as well go ahead and make it about something. With all due respect to my friends Jon Stewart and Stephen Colbert, it seems to me that if you truly wanted to come down on the side of restoring sanity and reason, you'd side with *the sane and the reasonable*—and not try to pretend the insanity is equally distributed in both parties. Keith Olbermann is right when he says he's not the equivalent of Glenn Beck. One reports facts; the other one is very close to playing with his poop. And the big mistake of modern media has been this notion of balance for balance's sake, that the left is just as violent and cruel as the right, that unions are just as powerful as corporations, that reverse racism is just as damaging as racism. There's a difference between a mad man and a madman.

Now, getting more than two hundred thousand people to come to a liberal rally is a great achievement that gave me hope, and what I really loved about it was that it was twice the size of the Glenn Beck crowd on the Mall in August—although it weighed the same. But the message of the rally as I heard it was that if the media would just stop giving voice to the crazies on both sides, then maybe we could restore sanity. It was all non-partisan, and urged cooperation with the moderates on the other side. Forgetting that Obama tried that, and found out there are no moderates on the other side.

When Jon announced his rally, he said that the national conversation is "dominated" by people on the right who believe Obama's a socialist, and by people on the left who believe 9/11 was an inside job. But I can't name any Democratic leaders who think 9/11 was an inside job. But Republican leaders who think Obama's a socialist? *All of them.* McCain, Boehner, Cantor, Palin . . . *all of them.* It's now official Republican dogma, like "Tax cuts pay for themselves" and "Gay men just haven't met the right woman."

As another example of both sides using overheated rhetoric, Jon cited the right equating Obama with Hitler, and the left calling Bush a war criminal. Except thinking Obama is like Hitler is utterly unfounded—but thinking Bush is a war criminal? That's the opinion of Major General Anthony Taguba, who headed the Army's investigation into Abu Ghraib.

Republicans keep staking out a position that is farther and farther right, and then demand Democrats meet them in the middle. Which now is not the middle anymore. That's the reason health-care reform is so watered down—it's Bob Dole's old plan from 1994. Same thing with cap and trade—it was the first President Bush's plan to deal with carbon emissions. Now the Republican plan for climate change is to claim it's a hoax.

But it's not—I know because I've lived in L.A. since '83, and there's been a change in the city: I can see it now. All of us who live out here have had that experience: "Oh, look, there's a mountain there." Governments, led by liberal Democrats, passed laws that changed the air I breathe. For the better. I'm *for them,* and not the party that is plotting to abolish the

EPA. I don't need to pretend both sides have a point here, and I don't care what left or right commentators say about it, I care only what climate scientists say about it.

Two opposing sides don't necessarily have two compelling arguments. Martin Luther King Jr. spoke on that mall in the capital, and he didn't say, "Remember, folks, those southern sheriffs with the fire hoses and the German shepherds, they have a point, too." No, he said, "I have a dream. They have a nightmare. This isn't Team Edward and Team Jacob."

Liberals, like the ones on that field, must stand up and be counted, and not pretend we're as mean or greedy or shortsighted or just plain batshit as them. And if that's too polarizing for you, and you still want to reach across the aisle and hold hands and sing with someone on the right, *try church.*

—November 5, 2010

T

TAMPACS

New Rule: Stop trying to scare me with your Mayan-calendar doomsday theories. I'm supposed to be terrified by counting the days on the Mayan calendar? Why? Is my Mayan girlfriend late for her Mayan period? If the Mayans could see the future, how come they couldn't get away from Cortés? Besides, we have much scarier things to worry about in 2012:

TANGO AND BASH

New Rule: If you send more than one news van to cover *Dancing with the Stars,* then you have to change your name from *Eyewitness News* to *Guess What, You Guys?*

TAT PATROL

New Rule: Now that everyone has a tattoo, it will now be considered rebellious to not have a tattoo. Seriously. I think the Jonas Brothers have tattoos now. I'm sure Mitt Romney is all inked up. Betty White has one across her back that says "Fuck the Police"—that I know for a fact.

TEA Rx

New Rule: If conservatives can call it Obamacare, every time a family is forced to file for bankruptcy due to a medical misfortune, or a sick child is dropped by his insurance company, or a patient dies because she can't afford surgery, we get to call it: "Tea Bagger Care."

TEXT MESSAGE

New Rule: Stop worrying that crackpots are inserting their dogma into Texas schoolbooks. Sure, replacing Thomas Jefferson with Phyllis Schlafly is troubling, but it's *Texas*. The only use Texans have for textbooks is to sit on them so they can get a better view of the football game. The last person to even notice Texas had schoolbooks was Lee Harvey Oswald.

THEATER NOT

New Rule: My friends who are actors must stop inviting me to their plays. The answer is no. I'm not busy, I just don't want to see your play. In fact, it's literally the very last thing in the world I want to do. If it becomes a movie, maybe I'll see it then. Not at the theater. But if it gets to Netflix, sure. You know me, anything to support the arts.

THIN BLUE WHINE

New Rule: Police cars have too many lights. The car on *Dragnet* had one light. On *Adam-12,* two lights. These days, police cars have blinking lights, rotating lights, strobe lights . . . Car 54, Where Are You? Studio 54, Where Are You? I don't know if I'm being arrested or invited to a rave.

THIN HIZZY

New Rule: If your home is built by Ikea, you're safer in the box it came in. Ikea is going into the home-building business, which on the upside means you'll be able to buy a five-bedroom house for $110. But when a hurricane hits, do you really want to be in a house made of corkboard and paper clips? Remember: Ikea is Swedish for "Where does this bolt go?"

TICKER SHOCK

New Rule: Stop calling what's happening to the financial markets "an adjustment." An adjustment is something you do in your sweatpants when your penis falls out of your underwear. This is "a clusterfuck."

TOKE MACHINE

New Rule: Until pot is legalized, you can't sell it in vending machines. There are three new medical marijuana machines in L.A., which goes against the natural order of getting high first and *then* buying shit from the vending machine. Call me old-fashioned, but if I'm going to break the law, I demand the full package, and that includes visiting a vaguely creepy dude named Skeet and wondering how long I have to "hang out" with him and his hollow-eyed husk of a girlfriend before I can take my weed and go.

GOODBYE, MR. CHIPS

New Rule: Someone in America must give me hope that this country can sacrifice anything to get anything done. I refer specifically to SunChips. You know SunChips—the corn-based snack you wolf down at the convenience store when you're high? Well, this year, they came out with something really cool: a biodegradable bag that won't contribute to the Texas-size swirls of plastic we now have in both the Atlantic and Pacific—and I couldn't wait to reward them with my business. Except now I can't. They stopped making this bag because there was a problem with it—it was loud. Like a porn star, it made a little too much noise when you stuck your hand in it. It crinkled in a disturbing fashion, like Keith Richards's face.

It's the sound of jackbooted eco-thugs taking away your inalienable right to be able to hear *Ice Road Truckers* perfectly while stuffing your face!

But unlike plastic, *this* bag would decompose into dirt instead of lying around for the next five hundred years to choke seagulls to death and destroy the ecosystem. Oh, sure, we could have made the ultimate sacrifice and, I don't know, poured the chips into a bowl . . .

Side note: In Canada, SunChips is keeping the non-earth-raping bag, because they're not a nation of crack babies, and they get it that sometimes you have to give up small things in order to make the world a better place. Except in America. Where "Have it your way" is the rule for everything, including volume on snacks. You think we're going to reform Social Security?

There's a lot of talk since the Republicans won the midterms that the *adults* are back in charge, having *adult* conversations about budget matters—for example, they say they want to keep the parts of the healthcare bill that people like, and repeal the parts that people don't like. Of course, it is the parts that people *don't* like that pay for the parts they *do* like. Yes, isn't it great to have the adults back in charge?

This is America. We don't have adult discussions. We have Twitter. If you have a problem with the baby talk that serves as our national dialogue, move to Finland—because ultimately it is our fault, not the politicians'. They just do what we tell them to do. If you showed Mitt Romney a poll that said he could win more votes if he became a woman named Mitteesha, he would get a weave and lop off his cock faster than you can say, "Is that thing sterilized?"

—November 12, 2010

TOMMY KNOCKER

New Rule: Since Tom DeLay has done only two things since leaving politics—*Dancing with the Stars* and now prison—somebody must tell him: There are easier ways to have sex with men.

TOOT BEER

New Rule: Stop trying to slip stimulants into my stimulants. Traces of cocaine have been found in Red Bull. Drinking Red Bull with cocaine is like watching golf on Xanax.

TOT AND BOTHERED

New Rule: Children's birthday parties must provide a little something for the grown-ups. And by something, I mean Jack Daniel's on ice with a twist. You can put it in a SpongeBob cup, I don't care. But I'm standing here in the blazing sun watching an out-of-work actor in a Spider-Man costume make balloon animals, and I need something to wash down the Vicodin I just stole from your medicine cabinet.

TOY STORY

New Rule: If we want to find a place to cut government waste, we must start with the DEA rubber duck. Yes, on the DEA's website you can buy a rubber ducky with a DEA badge and a cop's hat. Which I recommend doing, because they're a great place to hide your weed.

THE TREE AMIGOS

New Rule: Oil companies must stop with the advertisements implying they're friends of the environment. "At Exxon Mobil, we care about a thriving wildlife." Please—the only thing an oil executive has in common with a seagull is they'd both steal french fries from a baby.

TRUMP ROAST

New Rule: Whenever you think the Tea Party can't get any dumber, they get dumber. Now they're in love with Donald Trump. Because nothing says "We're serious about fiscal responsibility" quite like a billionaire whose corporations have filed for bankruptcy three times.

TRUTHER CONSEQUENCES

New Rule: Conspiracy theorists who are claiming that we didn't really kill Bin Laden must be reminded that they didn't think he did the crime in the first place. Come on, nutjobs, keep your bullshit straight: The towers were brought down in a controlled demolition by George W. Bush to distract attention from Hawaii, where CIA operatives were planting phony birth records so that a Kenyan named Barack Obama could someday rise to power and pretend to take out the guy we pretended took out the towers. And I know that's true because I just got it in an e-mail from Trump.

PEACE NIX

New Rule: The problem isn't that there's too little civility in government, it's that there's too much. President Obama's State of the Union speech is next week, and as you've probably heard, members of Congress have agreed, in response to the tragedy in Arizona, to break with the tradition of Republicans on one side of the room, Democrats on the other. Instead, they'll all sit together. Conservative next to liberal, gay next to straight, nerd next to jock . . . Oh, wait, that was an episode of *Glee*. In any event, the two parties are coming together, and they've agreed Joe Lieberman has to sit by himself.

America is such a mystery to me: A lunatic uses a Glock to shoot nineteen people, and our answer is: "Don't try to control guns or nuts, just be more polite." I'm just a hockey mom, but it seems to me when a madman kills people, the problem isn't the First Amendment. It's the Second.

In his big speech, President Obama said, "We should do everything we can to make sure this country lives up to our children's expectations." The first of which, I'm guessing, would be to live in a country where they don't get shot when they leave the house. That's what's important; who gives a damn if politicians mask their disdain for one another with forced niceties? They do already: "My good friend from the great state of Alabama." As if they're really good friends, or anyone outside Alabama thinks it's a great state.

Oh, it's a lovefest these days: Conservatives couldn't stop praising Obama's speech—of course, because it let them off the hook. The party of assault weapons didn't get blamed for the assault. Just like the party of oil didn't get blamed for the oil spill in the Gulf of Mexico. Like the party of deregulation skated on tanking the economy.

Again and again, Obama is given the opportunity to lay some richly deserved blame at the feet of the Republicans, and again and again he just can't do it, because he wants them to like him so badly—Conservatives, stop worrying, he can't be a Kenyan; he's a golden retriever. He's done every-thing he possibly could to appease you, short of using bleach.

And when Obama says "find common ground"—oh, here comes the bullshit now. Because whenever a Democrat seeks common ground, he always seems to find it right where the Republican was already standing. Ten years ago we had a ban on extended ammo clips so that people like this walking Thorazine ad couldn't kill supermarket crowds hassle-free. The Republicans killed the ban, and now the compromise is we can never get it back. I think the old word for that was "surrender."

Republicans—please note—are not taken in by the myth of common ground—they never move an inch on anything. Gun restrictions are al-ways bad, taxes are always too high, and there's nothing on earth that can't be improved by adding either Jesus or bacon. Sarah Palin knows fewer words than Koko the gorilla, but it's not a coincidence that two of them are "Don't retreat," and the other is "Reload."

—*January 21, 2011*

TURBAN OUTFITTERS

New Rule: If you still think Obama is a Muslim, you just might be a redneck. A Christian church in South Carolina has a sign out front that says, "Obama, Osama. Humm. Are they brothers?" No, in fact, they're not even related, which is more than I can say for the married couples in your church.

TURBAN RENEWAL

New Rule: Sikhs in America have to assimilate just a little more. Oh, I'm not talking about the do-rag, which is no sillier than a cowboy hat. But this week police had to break up a brawl at a Sikh temple in New York City involving swords and cricket bats. Whoa, fellas—this is America. We use guns here. Next time some shit starts at the temple, pull a Glock out of your turban and say, "Is there a motherfucking problem here?"

TWEENIE ROAST

New Rule: Science has to stop trying to determine why teens have sex. A new study links degrading lyrics to teen sex. Hey, Lab Coat, let me save you some time. You want to know why teens have sex? Because their teacher offered.

TWEET RELIEF

New Rule: My BlackBerry must find a better way to indicate that it's low on battery power than with a constant blinking light. Not to be rude, BlackBerry, but if you weren't using up all of that battery power letting me know that I'm low on battery power, I wouldn't be so low on battery power. Christ, you're a BlackBerry. If you're trying to tell me something—send me a text.

IRRITABLE BOWL SYNDROME

New Rule: Americans must realize what makes NFL football so great: socialism. That's right, the NFL takes money from the rich teams and gives it to the poorer ones . . . just like President Obama wants to do with his secret army of ACORN volunteers. Green Bay, Wisconsin, has a population of one hundred thousand. Yet this sleepy little town on the banks of the Fuck-if-I-know River has just as much of a chance of making it to the Super Bowl as the New York Jets—who next year need to just shut the hell up and play.

Now, me personally, I haven't watched a Super Bowl since 2004, when Janet Jackson's nipple popped out during halftime, and that split-second glimpse of an unrestrained black titty burned my eyes and offended me as a Christian. But I get it—who doesn't love the spectacle of juiced-up millionaires giving one another brain damage on a giant flat-screen TV with a picture so real it feels like Ben Roethlisberger is in your living room, grabbing your sister?

It's no surprise that some one hundred million Americans will watch the Super Bowl—that's forty million more than go to church on Christmas—suck on that, Jesus! It's also eighty-five million more than watched the last game of the World Series, and in that is an economic lesson for America. Because football is built on an economic model of fairness and opportunity, and baseball is built on a model where the rich almost always win and the poor usually have no chance. The World Series is like *The Real Housewives of Beverly Hills*. You have to be a rich bitch just to play. The Super Bowl is like Tila Tequila. Anyone can get in.

Or to put it another way, football is more like the Democratic philosophy. Democrats don't want to eliminate capitalism or competition, but they'd like it if some kids didn't have to go to a crummy school in a rotten neighborhood while others get to go to a great school and their dad gets them into Harvard. Because when that happens, "achieving the American dream" is easy for some and just a fantasy for others.

That's why the NFL literally shares the wealth—TV is their biggest source of revenue, and they put all of it in a big commie pot and split it thirty-two ways. Because they don't want anyone to fall too far behind. That's why the team that wins the Super Bowl picks last in the next draft. Or what the Republicans would call "punishing success."

Baseball, on the other hand, is exactly like the Republicans, and I don't just mean it's incredibly boring. I mean their economic theory is every man for himself. The small-market Pittsburgh Steelers go to the Super Bowl more than anybody—but the Pittsburgh Pirates? Levi Johnston has sperm that will not grow up and live long enough to see the Pirates in a World Series. Their payroll is $40 million; the Yankees' is $206 million. The Pirates have about as much chance at getting in the playoffs as a poor black teenager from Newark has of becoming the CEO of Halliburton.

So you kind of have to laugh—the same angry white males who hate Obama because he's "redistributing wealth" just love football, a sport that succeeds economically because it does just that. To them, the NFL is as American as hot dogs, Chevrolet, apple pie, and a second, giant helping of apple pie.

—January 29, 2011

U

UDDER NONSENSE

New Rule: The guys who wrote *Why Do Men Have Nipples?* must write another book called *If You Care, Then You're Gay.*

ULTRASOUND ADVICE

New Rule: If you can force a woman to look at a sonogram—to see what will happen if she has an abortion—you also have to let her see a crying baby, a bratty five-year-old, and a surly teenager to see what will happen if she doesn't. And you have to tell her it costs $204,000 to raise it until it turns eighteen, in 2028, where it will be a slave to the Chinese, in a radioactive world with no animals, fish, or plants.

CAKE BOSS

New Rule: If you think Michelle Obama is after your freedom because she merely suggests that our kids should exercise more and eat a little broccoli along with their lard, you don't deserve a place in the free market of ideas. You belong at the Cheesecake Factory. She's not Stalin because she notices your kids sweat Mountain Dew.

And yet this is bigger than America's ass—hard to believe, but indulge me. This is about the Tea Baggers' fundamental misunderstanding of the difference between freedom and the freedom to never be told anything—like avoid food served in a bucket. It's just a tradition that first ladies get to pick some mundane—and up until now, noncontroversial—cause to promote. Lady Bird Johnson: beautifying America. Barbara Bush had literacy. Betty Ford's was no hard liquor before ten a.m. Our previous first lady, Laura Bush, worked tirelessly against illiteracy, so between her efforts and her husband's, it was a tie. Hillary Clinton did pioneering work in looking the other way. I'm just saying, if your husband can convince you that the bra in the bed probably fell in at the mattress factory, you can overlook Hosni Mubarak.

When I look at a moon pie, I just see sugar and trans fat, not my constitutional freedoms. But Sarah Palin recently brought sugar cookies to a school as a protest against the government telling the school what to eat. Which of course it wasn't doing. Sean Hannity warned that we'd soon be paying fines for eating salt. Which isn't a problem for Hannity, who eats mostly boogers. When did the right wing become Joe Pesci over every little thing: "You sayin' I use too much salt? What am I, salty? Fuck you, I use too much salt—here, take some salt right down your throat!"

Forty years ago, when Lady Bird Johnson suggested we plant wildflowers to beautify the highways, the reaction was "Sounds like a neat idea!" not "Don't tell me what I can plant, bitch!"

I'm not saying the right objects to Mrs. Obama's efforts because the Tea

Baggers are stupid, or because they're hysterical, or because they hate black people. Though all of that is true. But what does it say about America that even a first lady suggestion has to be controversial—especially when she purposefully picked something no one could disagree with: Maybe we should send our kids outside to play. You know who else liked to send people places? Hitler. Rush Limbaugh makes a crack about this every week. Because who better to get your health advice from than a drug-addicted fat man. Rush, I have proof that no one in the government is forcing you to eat right and exercise: you.

—February 4, 2011

THE VILLAGE PAPAL

New Rule: Popes are supposed to love everybody. Pope Benedict has rejected France's new ambassador to the Vatican because he's gay and married to a man. The Pope said it just wouldn't be right to have a homosexual walking around his pretend country run by men in dresses. So stay away, you nasty gay Frenchman . . .

. . . or the Vatican guards in their adorable striped pantaloons will have their way with you!

VINYL VERDICT

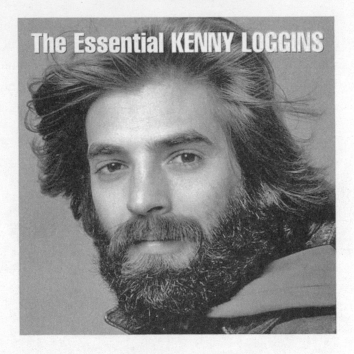

The Essential KENNY LOGGINS

New Rule: There's no such thing as essential Kenny Loggins.

VOLCANIC ASS

New Rule: You can't lecture people about economics if you own a volcano. Casino king Steve Wynn told Fox News: "Government has never increased the standard of living of one single human being in civilization's history. For some reason, that simple truth has evaded everybody." And then he put his elbow through a Picasso. Here's one way the government helped Las Vegas, just a little: We built the Hoover Dam. That's what makes all the little lights go on. So either start closing your casinos at sunset or buy the world's biggest flashlight. And shove it up your ass.

THREE FLOG NIGHT

New Rule: If your wife says, "Hurry up, we're going to be late for our Valentine's dinner," and you reply, "Just a minute, honey, I'm almost finished masturbating"—you might have a porn problem. I bring this up because there is a crisis in America: a full ninety-one percent of men can no longer get an erection without hearing the sound of a Mac booting up.

I made that statistic up, because statistics on porn are hard to come by, mainly because when you do a Google search for them you wind up looking at porn, and suddenly it's three hours later and the dog is starving. But it is true that in far too many marriages these days, the husband comes home from work and goes straight to the den to look at porn, while the poor wife is alone upstairs . . . Between him masturbating at his keyboard and her crying herself to sleep, who can keep that much Kleenex in the house?

I know what you're thinking: Bill Maher, anti-porn? No, I'm not anti-porn, I'm just saying, masturbation has its place—and that place should be plan B, when you can't get the real thing. For me, that was college. It filled the hole in me when I had no hole to fill. But now psychologists are telling us that for a sizable percentage of the men in America, masturbating to porn is plan A; doing it with your wife or girlfriend is more like a fallback option for when the power goes out.

What's worse, when someone spends twelve hours a day looking at porn, you build up a tolerance and you need more to get the same high. So you move on to fetish sites, and then weird Japanese porn, where a schoolgirl's being molested on a bullet train by Godzilla, and before you know it you're into the stuff that Germans like. Horrifying, slimy, violent ideas punctuated by the sounds of womanly sobbing. Like an interview with John Boehner.

And to be honest about our porn addiction—it's not that Americans are oversexed, it's that we are catastrophically lazy. We'd rather sit on the sofa and show our wing-wang to strangers on Chatroulette than go schlep out to Houlihan's and try to pick up a secretary who's had one too many mai tais. We've become a nation of cooch potatoes.

I'm getting action and I don't even have to brush my teeth! Real, actual sex? Not tonight, honey—I'm horny! It's amazing—for men, it took only a couple of decades between discovering that women can have orgasms and deciding that giving them one is just too much trouble.

—February 11, 2011

New Rule: Since the number-one cause of death in the Civil War was diarrhea—true—Civil War reenactors must do all their inspiring battle-field re-creations with a steaming load of crap in their pants. And if you think that sounds uncomfortable and unpleasant, try slavery.

I mention this because today marks the one hundred fiftieth anniversary of the inauguration of Jefferson Davis as president of the Confederacy, and that's when all the shooting and pooping started. And tomorrow in Montgomery, Alabama—in just one of many slavery shindigs around the South this year—the Sons of the Confederacy are sponsoring a march to "celebrate the Confederacy," part of a whole year of nostalgia, including battle reenactments, parades, and grand balls—which is what you have to have to convince people that there's nothing fucked up about celebrating slavery. Oh, I know, they're not celebrating slavery, they're celebrating a way of life: "Oh, I wish I was in the land of cotton"—because someone else was picking it!

I tell you, southerners—and I love them—have more disconnects than AT&T. And it started with Jefferson Davis—in his inauguration speech, he didn't once mention slavery. He just talked about "agriculture" and "resources," and then winked so much his wife thought he was sexting her by Morse code.

Now, I know you southerners have had a tough go at it. You lost the Civil War to the North. Reese Witherspoon to Hollywood. And the Dixie Chicks to Satan. And I'm not trying to offend my southern friends, mostly because you're on meth and packing heat, but underneath that trucker hat there's a plantation-size mental split going on. Because even the southerners who do the reenacting and lionize their slaveholding ancestors would tell you that they now think slavery was wrong. Then how could killing people to defend it have been right?

If my ancestors had fought for the right to abduct teenagers and force them into prostitution, I probably wouldn't reenact that on weekends with the cast of *Gossip Girl.* And why is it that the people who want to reenact the war are the losers? That's like doing sexual role-play and starting with, "Hey, remember that time I couldn't get it up? Let's relive that."

So I'm not saying that your great-great-grandpa Lucius Meriwether Cornpone didn't fight bravely at the Battle of Whogivesashit, but he was fighting on the wrong side. Just as I'm sure there were brave soldiers in Hitler's army, but I wouldn't start a restaurant called the Waffen Hut.

And all this talk about the "southern way of life" . . . please, I've been to the South. It's the same way of life we have over here. You watch TV, you go to the mall, you eat a soft pretzel, and you go home. You just do it *slower,* that's all. *Gone With the Wind* was just a movie. A movie made in Culver City. By Jews.

—February 18, 2011

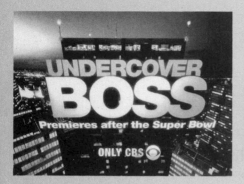 

New Rule: Television networks have to stop making shows that try and put a happy ending on America's enormous wealth disparity and instead make a show called *Shine My Shoes, Fuckface!* This is America, where the top four hundred people have more money than the bottom 150 million combined.

ABC gave us *Secret Millionaire,* which is like *Undercover Boss* but less intellectually taxing. In each episode, one of our richest one percent drops in on the wage slaves for a week and finds out that living on one hundred eighty-five bucks a week in America really blows, so they then anecdotally solve the wealth-gap problem by showering everyone with cash. It's like *Pretty Woman* if you were the whore.

It's amazing. TV used to give Americans the reverse fantasy: What if you, normal person, suddenly became a millionaire? Now it's "Oh, who are we kidding? You consider yourself lucky to hold on to your job deep-frying chicken parts, but how'd you like to be briefly *introduced* to a millionaire? Would you like that? You can even touch his garments!" And people watch this shit and find it inspirational. It's why they fawn over Donald Trump when he flirts with running for president every four years, even though he spends the rest of his time letting eighteen people kiss his ass before he fires all but one of them.

America's rich aren't giving you money. They're *taking* your money. Between the years 1980 and 2005, eighty percent of all new income generated in this country went to the richest one percent. Let me put that in terms even you fat-ass Tea Baggers can understand. Say one hundred Americans get together and order a one-hundred-slice pizza. The pizza arrives, they open the box, and the first guy takes eighty slices. And if someone suggests, "Why don't you just take seventy-nine slices?" *that's socialism*!

I know, it's just a TV show. But it does reinforce the stupid idea people have that rich people would love us, and share with us, if only they got to walk a mile in our cheap plastic shoes—but they're the reason the shoe factory moved to China. We have this fantasy that our interests and the interests of the super-rich are the same. Like somehow the rich will eventually get so full that they'll explode, and the candy will rain down on the rest of us. Like they're some kind of piñata of benevolence. But here's the thing about a piñata. It doesn't open on its own. You have to beat it with a stick.

Forget *Secret Millionaire*; I have a better idea for a show. Every week, one of the men responsible for the global financial meltdown is dropped into a poor neighborhood, and . . . And that's it. No cameras, we just leave him there. I call it *I'm Alan Greenspan. Get Me out of Here.*

—March 11, 2011

WART JESTER

New Rule: There doesn't have to be an app for everything. Researchers are developing a cell-phone app they say will diagnose STDs on the spot. So while you're downloading the Clash, you can get tested for the clap. Of course, the hard part isn't making your lovers understand the importance of safe sex—it's getting them to pee on your iPhone.

WEDDING SLASHERS

New Rule: If women stop making every movie about getting married, men will stop making every movie about killing you.

WEDGE ISSUE

New Rule: If you get to serve me a quarter-head of lettuce with dressing on it, which proves you *could* have made a salad but chose not to, then I get to pay you with an ATM receipt, which proves I have the money but you're not getting any.

WEED THE PEOPLE

New Rule: Telling me the pot is stronger doesn't scare me. The White House says that marijuana is stronger today than it's ever been, and that's why we need the crackdown, so we can return to the days when you needed to take ten hits to get high. This is what the drug war has come to. It's a war on "good shit." They're telling parents, "This is not the marijuana you remember." And I agree. But don't we want the best for our children? To leave them with a world that's better than the one we inherited? And that includes pot. So when you tell me today's pot has a higher THC content than ever before, I don't worry; I credit the American entrepreneur who made it. Against all odds, it's morning in America again.

BARRY, WHITE

New Rule: If the Republicans' idea of governing is just being against everything the president is for, then they have to change their name to the "I Know You Are, but What Am I?" party and nominate for 2012 a man who is the exact opposite of Obama. A fat, white, small-eared idiot who angers quickly, overreacts to everything, and can bowl 300, and who carries only one form of ID, his original birth certificate. A man so the antithesis of our current president that even his name is Barack Obama spelled backward. Say hello to the Republican Party's 2012 presidential candidate, Karab Amabo.

Now, before I give you the details about Karab Amabo, please understand, I'm not making this premise up. This week the Republican Party did a one-eighty on Libya so hard it drove John Boehner's tears back into his face. Totally ruining the leather. But let me tell you about Karab Amabo.

Amabo would be our first homeschooled president, and the first in his family to ever *not* graduate high school. After flunking out of bartending school, he spent years *dis*organizing communities, and wrote two books: a memoir, *Dreams from My Food Court,* and a policy book, *Thinking Is for Dummies.*

And what are his policies? Karab Amabo believes we should *increase* our dependency on foreign oil, and shrink the size of government until it performs only the most basic functions: killing Arabs, paying farmers to grow corn, and probing people at the airport. Karab Amabo believes abortion should be illegal, *especially* in the case of rape or incest, and he is so pro-life his slogan is "Life begins at erection."

Karab Amabo pledges to repeal the job-killing health-care bill, and to implement Amabocare, a comprehensive program that gives uninsured people with preexisting conditions the opportunity to walk it off.

Temperamentally, Karab Amabo believes America has had enough of "no drama Obama" and his measured, Vulcan logic. At the first sign of crisis, Amabo will pray, scream, shit his pants, and fly *Air Force One* into a mountain.

And what of Amabo's family? Karab Amabo's wife is a sour, ashen midget whose flaccid arms are so weak she can barely do her job, operating the deep fryer at Jack in the Box. The Amabos and their two sons go to church every four hours, and they have a meth lab where the White House garden used to be.

—March 25, 2011

WHAT ABOUT BLOB?

New Rule: You can't be president if you can't fit in the Oval Office. Governor Chris Christie says he's not running for president, but if he did, he'd definitely beat Obama. Which is like an eight-year-old saying, "I could kick your ass in tiddlywinks, I just don't *feel* like it." News flash, Governor Fat Bastard: Obama's approval rating in New Jersey is four points higher than *yours,* so I don't know what you're smoking. I mean, besides bacon.

WHITE-COLLAR CRIME

New Rule: Cocaine is not an aerosol. In Spain, a woman was arrested for trying to smuggle liquid cocaine disguised as spray starch. One sign your spray is actually cocaine: when your starched shirts have trouble staying hard.

WHY ME, GOURD

New Rule: Banks must stop putting up Halloween decorations and open up another teller window. You're a bank, not a college dorm room. Your service charges are scary enough. And while we're at it . . .

. . . stop trying to make my supermarket look like an old-fashioned farm stand. We get it. It's fall, and so the floor is now made of wood and the fruit is stacked in hay, but the other day my cart got stuck in a steaming pile of horseshit.

WING IT

New Rule: Arabs, when one of our planes goes down in your country, that doesn't mean you all have to rush over and stand on it. Maybe there's some cultural explanation, like Khadhafi didn't let you have jungle gyms and you're trying to get your childhood back. But I'm going to let you in on something: You're not striking a blow against the Great Satan. You're getting lead poisoning from General Dynamics.

WINTER'S BONEHEAD

New Rule: When you make stupid into an art form, it's not stupid anymore. We just found out that the "Sarah Palin" who writes Sarah Palin's Facebook page is a fake, but the real Sarah Palin has her own Facebook page under a fake name. And sometimes the real/fake Sarah Palin praises the work of the fake/real Sarah Palin. It's like *Inception* for hillbillies. There's also a rumor that she doesn't really need glasses, she just wears them to look smart. And when she has them on, Todd doesn't know she's Superman.

BRUCE ALRIGHTY

New Rule: Now that a Cheney, a McCain, and a Bush have come out to support gay marriage, it's your turn, Obama. Who are you waiting for, the state of Alabama? The Reverend Fred Phelps? Even sixty-three percent of *Catholics* are okay with gay marriage. But then again, they're used to being fed the body of a man by another man who's wearing a dress.

This month, America reached a milestone in its attitude toward gays: more than half the country—fifty-three percent— now supports gay marriage. Now, that still means that forty-seven percent of Americans are assholes. After all, if a poll found that forty-seven percent of Americans thought blacks shouldn't be able to marry a Kardashian sister, the Twittersphere would light up like Charlie Sheen just fell down a well. But still, this is remarkable progress, considering that it wasn't that long ago that just saying the words "gay marriage" made most Americans throw up in their cornflakes.

So I'd like to congratulate the leadership of the Democratic Party, who really stood up for what was right. I'd like to, but I can't, because other than Gavin Newsom, Dennis Kucinich, and that governor in New Jersey who went all *Brokeback Mountain* with his bodyguard, no Democrat would touch the issue with a ten-inch pole. It wasn't the Democrats who changed America on the issue—it was television, which in the last five years has gotten gayer than the British Navy. If there's one thing I know about Americans, it's that if they see something on TV, it makes it okay. And when they saw real gay couples standing on courthouse steps wearing the same ugly rented tuxedos that straight men wear to get married—suddenly, they realized that the gays were just like them: tacky and overweight.

Recently, Victoria Jackson, the oldest surviving member of *Saturday Night Live,* said the show *Glee* is "shoving the gay thing down our throats." Besides being the first funny thing she's said in twenty-five years, it's true. They *are* shoving the gay thing down America's throat, and it turns out

America got used to it surprisingly quickly. And that shouldn't shock anybody, because shoving things down America's throat is what the Republicans do all the time.

Unlike the Democrats, when Republicans believe in things that the public doesn't—their response is, "Fuck it, we'll *make* them believe." Like attacking Iraq to avenge 9/11. Like convincing a country that badly wanted health-care reform that they actually didn't want it. Like turning global warming into a hoax. That's what conservatives do—relentlessly push until the unthinkable becomes the consensus. The idea of blaming teachers for our financial crisis, which would have seemed completely lunatic a year ago, becomes the conventional wisdom.

Republicans don't run from unpopular stances, and they stand by their convictions. Stupid, ignorant, world-destroying convictions based on disproven economic fantasies and ancient books full of primitive morality and magic people—but convictions nonetheless.

—April 1, 2011

WORD IMPERFECT

New Rule: I don't care if white-trash America ever accepts that Barack Obama is president, but it's high time that my spellcheck did.

WORLD SERIES OF PORKER

New Rule: Competitive eating isn't a sport. It's one of the seven deadly sins. ESPN recently televised the U.S. Open of Competitive Eating, because watching those athletes at the poker table was just too damn exciting. What's next, competitive farting? Oh, wait, they're already doing that—it's called *The Howard Stern Show*.

WRAP SMEAR

New Rule: Someone has to explain to me the difference between eating the new McDonald's Big Mac Snack Wrap—which is basically a handful of burger chunks, lettuce, cheese, and sauce all glopped together on a tortilla—and eating out of the garbage.

WRECKS APPEAL

New Rule: If men can admit they watch NASCAR for the crashes, women can admit they watch fashion shows . . .

. . . to see skinny chicks fall on their asses.

CHARLIE DON'T SERF

New Rule: As long as we've got three wars going, America needs to add one more—a class war. It's time working Americans told Wall Street the same thing that the good people of Detroit told Charlie Sheen: "This is bullshit, and I want my money back."

Two interesting things are happening in America right now. Charlie Sheen—a millionaire armed with only a few catchphrases and two porn actresses who smell like ammonia—launched a self-pity tour because he can't have a TV show, while the Republicans—the party of millionaires—is shutting down the government because they can't have a tax-free world. As Paul Ryan says, "It's not a budget. It's a cause."

Like slavery. Like supporting one of the luckiest guys in the world in his quest to get all that's coming to him. Folks, if you go to a show and the guy onstage says, "Sorry, dude, I already got your money," you're not in on the joke. You *are* the joke.

You're not his friend, or one of his chosen people, and you're not going to *be* him someday in paradise if you drink his tiger blood. That's Jesus you're thinking of. This is the guy from the sitcom about making dirty jokes to a fat kid. You can know that a rock makes a shitty pet, but if you buy a pet rock, you're still an idiot. Ask your dentist—a shit-eating grin doesn't change the fact that you've been eating shit. That's the difference between being Charlie Sheen's girlfriend and Charlie Sheen's fan. If you're his girlfriend and you get fucked, he pays *you*.

And if you think a guy living large and rubbing your nose in it that you're *not* is funny, here's one you'll really love: You have to pay your taxes, and General Electric doesn't. That's right, GE, America's largest corporation, paid no taxes on $14 billion in profit. Why aren't people mad at them?

If I had to pick a phrase that encapsulates the American economy in the last decade, it surely would be: "I've already got your money, dude."

There's a law now forbidding credit-card companies from screwing you with fine print and sudden unjustified rate hikes—to which the credit-card companies said, "I already got your money, dude." Or maybe you lost your job in a recession caused by already rich people who bundled horseshit loans, and then took "too big to fail" pity money from Uncle Sam: "Already got your money, dude."

Americans need to have a Detroit moment, when they realize they're pooling their money and wasting it on the richest guy in the room. The richest one percent hoard an obscene amount of the wealth while the average American has to save up to eat at Red Lobster on his birthday. Wake up—because somehow, they're banging the porn stars, and you're getting the crabs.

—*April 8, 2011*

X-MEN

New Rule: If the water in your river makes the male fish grow vaginas, stay thirsty, my friend. Ninety percent of Washington, D.C.'s drinking water comes from the Potomac, a river so polluted with hormones it makes fish change sex. If I wanted to drink something that makes me grow a vagina, I'd order a wine cooler.

XXX FACTOR

New Rule: Stop trying to convince me that oral sex is the new handshake. For one thing, that would radically change the job requirements for the Walmart greeter. Plus, how would Hollywood starlets know when the introductions were over and the audition's begun?

THE PARTY OF STINKIN'

New Rule: Now that it's become clear that the Republicans, the fiscally conservative/strong on defense party, are neither fiscally conservative nor strong on defense, they have to tell us what exactly it is they're good at. Because it's not defense. 9/11 happened on your watch. And you retaliated by invading the wrong country. And you lost a ten-year game of hide-and-seek with Osama bin Laden. And you're responsible for running up most of the debt, which more than anything makes us weak. You're supposed to be the party with the killer instinct, but it was a Democrat who put a bomb in Khadhafi's bedroom and a bullet in Bin Laden's eye like Moe Greene in *The Godfather,* raising the question: How many Muslims does a black guy have to kill in one weekend before crackers climb down off his ass?

Let's look at some facts. For you Fox News viewers, feel free to turn down the sound until the flashing "FACTS" light at the bottom of your screen disappears. When Bill Clinton left office in 2001, the Congressional Budget Office predicted that by the end of the decade, we would have paid off the entire debt *and* have a $2 trillion *surplus*. Instead, we have a $10.5 trillion public debt, and the difference in those two numbers is mostly because the Republicans put tax cuts for the rich, the prescription drug plan, and two wars on the layaway plan, and then bailed on the check. So . . . so much for fiscal responsibility.

But, hey, at least they still had the defense thing, right? The public still believed Republicans were tougher when it came to hunting down dark-skinned foreigners with funny-sounding names. But Bush had seven years to get Osama bin Laden. He didn't. He got Wesley Snipes. Only six months after 9/11, Bush said he didn't spend that much time on Bin Laden and that he was "no longer concerned" about him. Just as he wasn't before 9/11, when he blew off that mysterious, inscrutable memo titled "Bin Laden Determined to Attack Inside the U.S." In under a year, Bush went from

"Who gives a shit?" to "Wanted: Dead or Alive," and back to "Who gives a shit?" Why focus on the terrorist who reduced Wall Street to rubble when you can help Wall Street reduce the whole country to rubble?

In 2008, the candidates were asked, if they knew for sure that Bin Laden was in Pakistan, would you send our guys in without permission to get him? McCain said no, because "Pakistan is a sovereign nation." Obama said yes, he'd just do it, and McCain called him "naïve." Who's being naïve, Kay? And why can't you just admit that Barack Obama is one efficient, steely nerved, multitasking black-ninja gangsta president? In one week, he produced his birth certificate, comforted disaster victims, swung by Florida to say hey to Gabby Giffords, did stand-up at the Correspondents' Dinner, and then personally rappelled into Bin Laden's lair and put a Chinese star through his throat without waking up any of his thirteen wives. That's how it went down. I saw it on MSNBC.

Thirty percent of the country will always vote Republican—I'm just asking why. Yes, paranoia, greed, and racism are fun, but . . . it's like when you see someone driving a Mercury. You think: "Did that person really wake up one day thinking, 'You know what car I want to drive? A Mercury Mariner.'" No, you assume he knows someone who sells them. Or he was molested by a Kia dealer as a child.

I know this all sounds like harsh truth, but Republicans are supposed to be the party of harsh truths. Like there's no such thing as a free lunch. And speaking of lunch, I think Obama just ate yours.

—*May 6, 2011*

THY WILL BE GUN

New Rule: If you're a Christian who supports killing your enemies and torture, you have to come up with a new name for yourself. Last week, as I was explaining why I didn't feel at all guilty about Osama's targeted assassination, I made some jokes about Christian hypocrisy, and since then, strangers have been coming up to me and forcing me to have the same conversation. So let me explain two things: (1) No, I'm not Matthew McConaughey. He surfs a longboard. And (2) capping thine enemy is not exactly "what Jesus would do." It's what Suge Knight would do.

For almost two thousand years, Christians have been lawyering the Bible to try and figure out how "Love thy neighbor" can mean "Hate thy neighbor" and how "Turn the other cheek" can mean "Screw you, I'm buying space lasers." Martin Luther King Jr. gets to call himself a Christian because he actually practiced loving his enemies, and Gandhi was so fucking Christian he was Hindu. But if you rejoice in revenge, torture, and war—hey, that's why they call it the weekend—you cannot say you're a follower of the guy who explicitly said, "Love your enemies," and "Do good to those who hate you." The next line isn't "And if that doesn't work, send a titanium-fanged dog to rip his nuts off." Jesus lays on that hippie stuff pretty thick, with lines like "Do not repay evil with evil" and "Do not take revenge on someone who wrongs you." Really. It's in that book you hold up when you scream at gay people.

And—not to put too fine a point on it—nonviolence was kind of Jesus' trademark. Kind of his big thing. To not follow that part of it is like joining Greenpeace and hating whales. There's interpreting—and then there's just ignoring. It's just ignoring if you're for torture, as are more Evangelical Christians than any other religion. You're supposed to look at that figure of Christ on the cross and think, "How could a man suffer like that and forgive?" not "Romans are pussies; he still has his eyes." If you go to a baptism and hold the baby under until he starts talking, you're missing the message.

Like, apparently, the president, who says he gets scripture on his Black-Berry first thing every morning, but who said on *60 Minutes* that anyone who would question that Bin Laden deserved assassination should "have their head examined." Hey, Fox News, you missed a big headline: "Obama Thinks Jesus Is Nuts." To which I say, hallelujah, because my new favorite government program is surprising violent religious zealots in the middle of the night and shooting them in the face. Sorry, Head Start. You're number two now. But I can say that because I'm a non-Christian—just like most Christians.

I'm just saying logically, if you ignore every single thing Jesus commanded you to do, you're not a Christian. You're just auditing. You're not Christ's followers, you're just fans. And if you believe the earth was given to you to kick ass on, while gloating, you're really not a Christian. You're a Texan.

—*May 13, 2011*

Y

YAHOO SIRIUS

New Rule: News radio stations must find sponsors for something other than mortgages, tax problems, bankruptcy, erectile dysfunction, and garage doors. It sounds like a *Jeopardy!* category: Things in a suicide note. "Darling, please forgive me, but there was no other way out, after the mortgage drove me into bankruptcy, and the IRS slammed my penis in the garage door."

YANKS, BUT NO YANKS

New Rule: Massage parlors must stop offering happy endings. I'd like to get a massage, but I'm terrified that at the end of it, the middle-aged Chinese lady is going to grab my junk with her rough peasant hands and work it like a piece of farm machinery. It's my *back* that's sore, not my penis. Besides, the whole point of hand jobs is that you can do them yourself.

CORPORATE PROPHET

New Rule: Contrary to what Republican candidates always sell, business experience does not make someone a good president. Honestly, do you people really want to get in this argument with me? George Bush had business experience. There. I win. Now shut up before I mention Donald Trump, the business genius whose companies have filed for bankruptcy three times. By the way, you know what makes a really great businessman? When your father has $400 million and dies. Or, as Trump calls it, "The Art of the Deal."

Yesterday, Mitt Romney announced he's running for president, and last week at a rally in Iowa almost two hundred people showed up, leading people to ask, what is the secret to Romney's almost Lady Gaga–like appeal, that two hundred Iowans would brave a partly sunny day with temperatures in the low seventies just to get a glimpse of the man? Is it because he looks like a model in the 1983 Montgomery Ward catalog? That's part of it. But his big claim to fame is that he's a *businessman*. And in America, saying you're a businessman automatically makes you better than anyone who's not a businessman. Obama never ran a business; he was a community organizer. Helping poor people. Where's the money in that? Stupid loser.

Romney, on the other hand, is all business. You get the impression that he delays orgasm by calculating interest rates. In his speech, Romney said, "Unlike President Obama, I know how jobs are created and how jobs are lost." Yeah, especially the lost part. Here's what Romney's former company, Bain Capital, does: It buys companies and revamps them by "cost cutting"—otherwise known as "firing people"—and then sells them for a profit.

Mitt's other business success story besides Bain Capital is Staples. Yes, that Staples. The store that sells you ink cartridges. The store you put off going to for as long as you can. The store with zero décor and a flickering fluorescent light that makes you think, "Has my life really come to this?"

You see, businessmen generally make lousy political leaders because government isn't about turning a profit, it's about taking care of the things that shouldn't have to turn a profit. You can't make everything better with "business." Business can't turn coal into diamonds, or crap into food. That's soy sauce.

So, Mitt, instead of pointing out your business experience, try using the fact that you were the governor of Massachusetts, the most educated state in the country, and your main accomplishment was universal health care. Then again, you're trying to appeal to the Republican base, so you'll have to do that in a way that avoids mention of Massachusetts, universal health care, or smart people.

—June 3, 2011

YOU, ME, AND DUPRÉ

New Rule: If your news organization's website has more than three pictures of Eliot Spitzer's hooker on it, you're a porn site. The only difference: On a porn site, "Spitzer" is a verb.

YOU'VE GOT BAIL

New Rule: I understand that we had to bail out this insurance company.

But if the one with the Cockney lizard gets in trouble, just let it die.

HAND SOLO

New Rule: If you're going to be the pathetic, laughing-stock center of a tawdry, lie-riddled sex scandal, at least get laid. Congratulations, Congressman Shinytits69: In a world of politicians doing everything from having babies with the maid, leaving their wives on their deathbeds, and hiking the Appalachian Trail, you're guilty of the most humiliating indiscretion of all: You didn't get any. Talk about Democrats being ineffectual! Edwards and Clinton banged butterfaces, and that's embarrassing enough—but you came up with just . . . your hand. Your name shouldn't even be Weiner, you don't deserve it—Weiners are for closers—your name should be Anthony Hand.

At his press conference, Congressman Weiner was talking about his online flirtations, and at one point he ejaculated, "They are all adults, at least to the best of my knowledge." Oh, Anthony, it's the Internet. There's no such thing as the best of your knowledge. You know that naked coed you've got on the line, the one with tits that just won't quit? This is her:

How is talking to this guy online better than old-school whacking off? Say what you want about a box of Kleenex and the July *Playboy,* but when you finish, it doesn't call Andrew Breitbart.

I guess I just don't get the appeal of sexting, and phone sex, and all that cyber-jacking the kids are into these days when they're not listening to their hippity-hop records. Call me old-fashioned, but when I have sex I like to have the other person in the room. I find that it helps create a feeling of intimacy.

People say, "Bill, don't knock phone sex till you've tried it." I've tried it. True, it was with a customer-service rep from the gas company, but still. I gave it a shot. And you know what? It's not sex. It's not even a little bit like sex. It's just talking. Even during actual sex, talking is fairly superfluous. Saying "Do me, do me" when I am at that very moment doing you is neither helpful nor essential to the overall experience. And that's all cyber-sex is: an annoying person saying "Do me, do me" while you're a thousand miles away, trying to maintain an erection while the cat walks across the keyboard.

Thanks to you, Congressman Weiner, there is now a new low in what passes for a sex scandal—JFK got Marilyn Monroe. John Edwards got a love child. You got mail. Say what you will about Bill Clinton, but at least when he whipped out his dick on a woman, she didn't have to wait for it to stop buffering.

—June 10, 2011

Z

ZINE-OPHOBIA

New Rule: Stop trying to make your magazine interactive. *Time* maga-zine keeps telling me that if I want to read more about a story, go to their website. Here's a better idea: Put the rest of the story *in the magazine.* You know, like you used to do before the Internet? I know you have a website that you're really proud of, but I'm on the toilet.

ZIP COLD

New Rule: As long as they're thinking of dropping Saturday service, the Post Office can go ahead and just close altogether. Since about 1998, no one in America has gotten anything in the mail but catalogs, bills, Christ-mas cards, and anthrax. And I hate Christmas cards. At least when you get anthrax you don't think, "Oh, shit, now next year I have to send them anthrax."

New Rule: If you think the Republican presidential candidates can't possibly get any lamer, then you haven't met the new Republican flavor of the month: Rick Perry. If you're not familiar with Rick, he took over as governor of Texas from George W. Bush, who's now referred to as "the smart one." He carries a gun even when he's jogging, he wears cowboy boots with a suit, and the boots say, "Come and take it," which sounds kind of gay. And he threw such a tantrum when Obama won, he actually talked about Texas seceding from the union. Because that's what America needs: a president of the United States who's not really sold on the whole "United States" concept.

Rick Perry rented out a seventy-thousand-seat football stadium in Houston for something called The Response—which sounds like a home pregnancy test but actually is, to quote the governor, "a Christian prayer service to provide spiritual solutions to the many challenges we face as a nation." Or, as stadium employees are calling it, Batshit Day. I guess the idea is to get together in a big group and pray all at once; that way, the signal is stronger and God doesn't lose you when he's going through a canyon.

But here on Planet Reality, may I point out that there are no such things as "spiritual solutions" to national problems. If that's where we are as a country, if our official government policy is "Yee-haw, Jesus, take the wheel"—then we're dead already. On his Jesuspalooza website, Perry writes, "There is hope for America. It lies in heaven, and we will find it on our knees," and "Some problems are beyond our power to solve." What? I thought we were the can-do people. And if Perry thinks only God can solve our problems, then why is he even *in* government? Why doesn't he just stay at home and light a bunch of candles, like Sissy Spacek's mom in *Carrie*?

Here's an opposing view: Not only are our problems *not* "beyond our power to solve," they're actually fairly easy to solve. You have a giant budget deficit, like Perry has in Texas? Raise taxes. Federal tax revenues haven't been this low since 1950—and *that,* plus two wars and a recession, is the reason we have a huge deficit. It's not because God's angry over the gay kissing on *Glee*. It doesn't require prayer to solve it; it requires a calculator.

Politicians like to say, "We need new ideas." Bullshit—"new ideas" is just a secular version of "spiritual solutions"—something that's going to magically fix everything. What "new idea" is going to solve our health-care crisis? A magic pill that makes obese children crap out gold bricks? We don't need "new ideas," we need the balls to implement the ideas we already know work: cut corporate welfare, slash the defense budget, tax the rich, support the strong unions that created a middle class in the first place, build infrastructure, and take the profit out of health care.

By the way, Rick Perry isn't just talking when he says "spiritual solutions." Back in April, faced with a devastating drought, Rick did what any solutions-oriented twenty-first-century civil servant would do. He proclaimed a Day of Prayer for Rain. Because we're ancient Mayans now. Of course, the drought only got worse. In the words of Sister Mary Ignatius, God answers all your prayers. And sometimes the answer is no.

—June 17, 2011

PHOTO CREDITS

Page 54: Top: Robert Voets/CBS/Landov

Page 54: Bottom: AP Photo/Doug Mills

Page 67: Top: Ocean/Corbis

Page 67: Bottom: RNT Productions/Corbis

Page 69: Trae Patton/NBCU Photo Bank via AP Images

Page 73: AP Photo/J. Scott Applewhite

Page 74: AP Photo/Beth A. Keiser

Page 79: Gilbert Tourte/Reuters/Landov

Page 93: Stephen M. Dowell/MCT/Landov

Page 94: PacificCoastNews.com

Page 95: Reuters/Landov

Page 97: AP Photo/Jennifer Graylock

Page 121: AP Photo/Reed Saxon

Page 126: AP Photo

Page 128: AP Photo/Stephan Savoia

Page 129: Gary C. Caskey/UPI/Landov

Page 130: Jason Reed/Reuters/Landov

Page 138: WireImage

Page 143: Reuters/Corbis

Page 148: AP Photo/Colin E. Braley

Page 151: Pablo Martinez Monsivais/UPI/Landov

Page 152: Yuriko Nakao/Reuters/Landov

Page 153: Arnaud Finistre/Maxppp/Landov

Page 163: AP Photo/Yin Bogu, Pool

Page 173: AP Photo/Marcio Jose Sanchez/File

Page 174: MAI/Landov

Page 176: Simon Battensby

Page 181: Top: AP Photo/Jennifer Graylock

Page 181: Bottom: Nik Wheeler/Corbis

Page 182: AP Photo/Minnesota Public Radio/Bob Collins

Page 183: AP Photo/Shiho Fukada

Page 186: Chicago/PA Photos/Landov

Page 194: AP Photo/Charlie Neibergall

Page 195: Getty Images

Page 206: Top: AP Photo/Jae C. Hong

Page 207: AP Photo/Alastair Grant

Page 231: AFP/Getty Images

Page 237: David Silpa/UPI/Landov

Page 239: AP Photo/Ben Curtis

Page 242: WireImage

Page 244: Bottom: Getty Images

Page 246: Bettmann/Corbis

Page 262: AP Photo/Jose Luis Magana

Page 264: AP Photo/Rich Schultz

Page 267: Philip Gould/Corbis

Page 272: Kelly Redinger/Design Pics/Corbis

Page 274: Jason Reed/Reuters/Landov

Page 279: AP Photo/J. Scott Applewhite/File

Page 303: Alessandra Benedetti/Corbis

Page 317: AP Photo/Julio Cortez

Page 318: Top: Chuck Savage/Corbis

Page 318: Bottom: Mark Bolton/Corbis

Page 319: Suhaib Salem/Reuters/Landov

Page 324: Stefano Rellandini/Reuters/Landov

Page 342: AP Photo/Richard Drew

Page 343: Mark Hayes and Digital Vision

Page 348: MCT via Getty Images